Clear the Mind for Success

Learning Meditation for Business

by

Brad J. Liski

Second Edition, 2017

Printed in Canada

ISBN: 978-0-9878194-6-8

Eaglet Publishing
#230-4321 Still Creek Drive
Burnaby, BC, Canada V5C 6S7

Table of Contents

Foreword

I have always been interested in meditation, but I generally only practiced it when I was in yoga class. However, when I assumed the role of president in our family business a few years ago, I became more interested in meditation and the benefits of a regular practice.

In my personal experience, I have found that meditating and quieting my mind has given me a method to ground myself and connect to my spirit. As a result, it provides me with the clarity to make difficult decisions, a fresh perspective on issues, as well as the ability to come up with creative solutions to business challenges. I also find meditation helps me control my reactions to situations and allows me to respond more calmly to emotional and stressful situations, both personally and professionally.

And I'm not alone. Many global leaders attribute no small part of their professional success to meditation. Steve Jobs practiced it and more and more leaders—ranging from Oprah Winfrey to Salesforce CEO Marc Benioff to LinkedIn CEO Jeff Weiner—have been taking note of the benefits of meditation and incorporating it into their daily routine. Known benefits include lower stress levels, improved cognitive functioning, creative thinking and productivity, and even improved physical health.

If you are considering exploring or learning more about the practice of meditation, Brad Liski's book, *Clear the Mind For Success, Learning Meditation for Business*, is an excellent introduction to meditation.

This easy-to-read book is accessible, practical and entertaining. As a successful entrepreneur himself, Brad is a learned practitioner of meditation and shares his knowledge in a fun format that will introduce you to the power of the practice.

Clear the Mind For Success will help you understand how to meditate, listen to your body, lead with empowerment and much more. This book is clearly written and will help you as it has helped me.

Samantha Legge, MBA
President,
Canada Wide Media Limited

Introduction

The story you are about to read is a business fable intended to introduce how meditation may be able to help your business.

The people are all fictional and they are a compilation of my personal experiences as well as those I have witnessed in others. Though Peter's journey is condensed for literary effect, my personal journey with learning meditation spanned over a decade. Each person will travel at their own pace if they so desire to integrate meditation into their business life.

The lessons are based on several of my teachers throughout my journey. Each topic is very lightly skimmed and a deeper understanding should and can be gained through dedicated lessons from a professional instructor. This book and the teachings in it are not a definitive guide to meditation in business and we make no claims that following these methods will provide you with answers you may seek nor the affect finding those answers may have on you, your business or your personal life.

Special thanks to the many people who have helped me bring this book to fruition. To Shannon, a business partner who introduced me to meditation and Bill who gave me the courage and showed me how to bring the message to the masses. To R.K. who pushed me to improve the lessons for basic understanding. To Anita who would not let me rest until I finished the book, making sure I did not lose sight of the goal. Last, but not least, to my family who not only endured five years of "Can you read this part?" but many more years of my struggle to clear my own mind and get on with my purpose.

Chapter One – Three Words

The contract loomed on his desk, wanting to be signed. He'd waited months for this and yet he found himself staring at the ½" thick stack of papers. "Why does every contract have a blue paper triangle stapled in the corner?" was all Peter could think of. His entrepreneurial career had seen countless documents like this one. Owning his first business at the age of 18, he now found himself in his early 40s wondering if the journey was worth it. He hadn't taken the easy road. Ambition and money got the better of him at an early age when he returned home the summer of his freshman year. Though he went back to university time and time again over the years, he found the training he'd received at his own school of hard knocks put his ego ahead of the professors' teachings. Peter smirked as he remembered how naive he was; thinking that at such a young age that he knew everything there was to know about business.

The next two decades flashed through his mind in a matter of moments - a parade of successes and failures through the 20 companies he has bought, sold, started, closed. The Win and Loss columns were both full but who could really distinguish wins from losses now that he looked back at it all. "So many times I thought I'd lost but it's now clear that some of those were actually wins." Peter said aloud in his empty office.

'Peter Strikman, Businessman': those three words were glaring at him on the first page of the contract. Just him. No one else was on the hook with him. He was alone this time.

With that thought he looked around his corner executive suite. The granite desk, a custom manufacturing error from his 11th company turned into a 10 foot boomerang shaped desk. The 40 inch monitor buzzing as the metrics poured in from the various things an executive measures. The signed Muhammad Ali glove hanging in its monster frame on the wall. "First Round, First Minute" inscribed on the plaque as *The Greatest* stood over Sonny Liston. Peter's mind drifted back many years to when he bought that glove. That was when times were good with Tim, his current business partner and the reason this contract had arrived.

"Oh yes... the contract" Peter sighed heavily as he snapped back into the moment. "What got so messed up to put me here? Really, is this the right thing to do?"

Staring at the contract he read the document's title:

Receivership Settlement Agreement

Three final, definitive words. Not the words he thought he would see when he started out to save this company. He saw this as the retirement venture. The one that would give him and his family what they needed for the rest of their lives. He would stop buying and selling businesses like baseball cards, settle down and have just this one company. In the end, he believed the three-word document he'd be looking at would be... *Initial Public Offering.* But that was not the case today.

Breaking his stare, he realized that the choice was now his and his alone. He did as he'd been taught, he closed his eyes, took a deep breath and remembered exactly why he'd taken this path and why he found himself here. The images and conversations were vivid in his mind as he relived the last four months...

Chapter Two – Good Money

"We are not putting more money into the company!" Peter yelled at Tim, who was clearly not hearing Peter's concerns. "We have to cut costs, not just keep shoring up the losses. You know as well as I do that I'm the last person to say tomorrow won't be better, but tomorrow won't be better!"

"You haven't been through this, Peter. It'll come around." Tim said, offering his usual I-am-wise-beyond-your-years response. Though Tim and Peter were partners and Peter was President, Tim held corporate control – an arrangement much-regretted by Peter. He clearly placed too much faith in Tim's personal promises. Tim continued, "We can't cut any more. You're cutting into the meat now. How are we going to operate?" Tim had been around for more years than Peter and his decades of experience in this industry were keeping him locked on his position. He slicked back his white, wavy hair with a swipe of his labourer's hands: "We just have to sell more."

Peter lit up like a Christmas tree. "Are you kidding me? That one again? Do you even own a TV? We're in a recession! And we're a non-essential service in a disposable-income market. We've been through this a thousand times. The numbers are obvious. The reality is just that... reality. Face it!"

Peter's temper and frustration were hitting a peak, threatening to send a list of every little thing Tim had done over the past two years spewing from his lips, but he dug deep into his soul and found the strength to hold back. Peter liked the company, liked the employees, liked the industry and saw great potential for the 25 year-old entity to turn around and be great. He knew full well that if he'd let go with all guns blazing that everything would come crashing to a halt and the inevitable shut-down would soon follow.

"It's all right there, Tim" Peter pointed to the Strategic Plan created and maintained for the two years he'd been here. "And to help, I've even graphed out how much money you'd invested before I arrived. It shows how - even though we stopped the free-fall with my initial cuts as well as the 30 percent increase in sales - we can't just sit idly by. It's not enough. You get these every quarter, Tim. What is there not to understand?" Peter was trying desperately to illustrate the reality.

"But you can't look at it that way." Tim replied, flipping through the quarterly results but clearly not knowing or caring what the graphs showed.

Peter, unlike Tim, had been here before. He knew the signs and though he was younger, his experiences were greater. Peter also knew that there was an answer to fixing this company - he just couldn't see it. His anger had boiled over and clouded his mind.

Lisa the bookkeeper knocked at the door to give Tim some reports he'd asked for and they chatted for a moment or two. Peter's brain just wouldn't shut off. He drifted into a place where his mind started a conversation with itself. 'These are some ugly times, man. Why can't he see this isn't like the past? Why don't I just walk away? What's keeping me here? My investment isn't even a tenth of what Tim's squandered. If he won't listen, why don't I just let this thing crash and burn and bury him? I don't need the job and my other companies could use my attention. Why am I hanging on?' The internal struggle continued as Peter remembered all the outside influences that he faced. News was hitting him from one side...clients' tales of woe from another...friends, family, even coffee shop chatter...and the story was always the same: things are bad. Different theories, different fingers pointed at different people, different spots of optimism and different doubts too. 'I'm not a negative guy; I've always been thought of as optimistic, sometimes overly-optimistic, but these are tough times. I've read all the Think-Big-Be-Big, You-Can-Do-It books. I've spent countless hours listening to tapes about the power of positive thinking... I know there's an answer! Why can't I just see it clearly and get this guy to understand? There must be a way to shut off this chatter and get a clear thought.'

Peter broke from his trance and said abruptly, "Tim, I have to go to a meeting. You two figure out what you need to figure out. I'll call you later." With that, Peter left without even waiting for a response. He headed straight for the front door, without any of his usual "Everything okay?" to the team. He didn't even pause at the front desk to say "Have a great night." The entire staff knew something wasn't right.

Chapter Three – Going Golfing

The question plagued Peter for days. His thoughts were in overdrive and his internal conversation continued, 'Why can't I see the answer? Why can't I drive it home to Tim?' He struggled to find the solution but whenever he came close, something else would happen. Some other department, some client…someone would throw a wrench into the spokes and he'd lose his train of thought. He scoured his notes, but found them scrambled with incomplete words and strategies. It seemed the more he thought about how to survive, the worse things got.

Then on Sunday, with no fight left in him, he did what every good executive struggling to get through the recession did. He plunked himself down on the couch and turned on the TV. Looking either for mindless programs or something inspiring - one of the two and he didn't care which. Instead, he tuned in to the final round of the PGA Masters. "Great!" Peter said sarcastically. "I get to watch some lucky morons smack a ball around and get paid ridiculous amounts of money. That'll make me feel better...NOT!" The highlights recapped the past 10 years of the PGA and the same few people always appeared at the top of leader boards. Peter wondered: 'Why were these men so amazingly different? What's their secret to success?'

His memory came to his rescue and something snapped in Peter's mind. "Golfers! They have the answer!" He faintly recalled a long-ago interview with a young golfer who was taking off like a rocket. That same golfer was the top name on the leader boards of the past decade.

"What makes you successful?" the interviewer asked the aspiring golfer in his now branded Sunday red golf shirt.

"It's simple - it's meditation," he replied. "I meditate on the perfect swing with the perfect tempo and simply focus on one thing and one thing only... making the shot."

"That's it!" Peter screamed jumping from the leather couch that still bore the imprint of his back.

"What's going on?!" Peter's wife, Marie, screamed back as their kids ran around the corner to see what their dad was screaming about.

"That's what I need." Peter yelled at them.

Staring at the TV, his family didn't see the new workout equipment or handyman tool they'd expected. All they saw were the golf highlights.

"You want to be a golfer?" Sam, Peter's 11 year-old son asked.

"No!" said Peter, "I want to focus. I need to focus!"

Looking around the room it was clear to Peter that his entire family felt he'd lost his mind. They understood the pressures he'd been under. In fact, Jessica, Peter's 14 year-old daughter, understood the recession better than most business people. And Marie? Well, she'd been with Peter through all the toils and troubles of this latest partnership, so she simply smiled, and turned back to what she was doing.

"I need to meditate!" Peter continued, rambling. "Pro golfers can do it... that's what make them shut out the outside noise. They meditate!"

Jessica did her eye-rolling thing, turned and left the room to join her mom. Sam, still amazed at the volume of his dad's enthusiasm asked: "What are you talking about?"

"Sam, do you understand what I am saying?"

"No Dad, that's why I said 'What are you talking about?'" his 11 year-olds clarity was refreshing to Peter, forcing him to smile for the first time in a while.

"Meditation is the answer to shutting down the outside noise and deciding what to do with the business."

"Okay Dad," said Sam from the couch where he kept his eyes fixed on the TV. "Who's winning?"

Peter smirked at Sam's response and gave him a hug. Happy to be sitting on a couch with his son, he realized he just might have the answer to the problem.

As the next few days went by Peter saw more and more evidence of meditation and began to think everyone on the planet had experienced the same revelation. Wandering the streets, he saw ad after ad featuring women in yoga poses, looking like they hadn't a worry in the world.

"I need that peace of mind." Peter said, staring at yet another poster. "I want to be that calm."

Peter, in the deepest part of his heart, felt that if he could calm his mind, he'd see clearly and find the answer. Fully determined to become calm, Peter headed to the local book store for a great book on meditation. Chest out, eyes focused and walking confidently, he entered the store. "Look out world! Peter's here to get the answers!" Both doors swung open as if for an emperor in all his finery. It'd been a few years since Peter had been in a book store and even then, he'd rarely gone past the business aisle. He spotted a young man wearing the store's corporate colours and sporting a stylish apron and strode purposefully toward him.

"Hello Kevin." Peter always read nametags as he approached people knowing that the sweetest sound a person can hear is the sound of their own name. His sales training was kicking and boosting his confidence. "Where can I find a book on meditation?"

"They start on aisle seven," said Kevin.

Peter headed for aisle seven, anticipating a simple See/Grab/Buy - his kind of shopping. But as he approaches the aisle, he had his first shock. "There are three aisles of meditation books?" Peter was stunned. "Are you kidding me?"

Thirty minutes and two lattes later, Peter had picked up countless books, and put back the same number.

"This is ridiculous," grumbled Peter, feeling dejected and confused. The drive home was slow and depressing.

"Maybe it's just time to shut the company down. Call it quits and tell everyone we tried." He had no audience in his empty car. The soliloquies were becoming more frequent and Peter actually caught himself smiling ruefully.

The next morning Peter had his determination back. It's amazing what a good scotch and a night's sleep will do. This time he went to the real source of information... Google. Typing in: "Meditation", he found just what you'd expect: 32,700,000 responses. "Arrgh" Peter said to the computer. He was beginning to understand now that meditation was definitely not an abstract concept. Narrowing his search, he typed: *Meditation teaching for business applications.* Only 10,400 responses. 'That's better!' he thought.

Topping the list was: 'Ling HO – Meditation Master'.

Said Peter: "Google can't be wrong."

With a dramatic pause, Peter clicked on the link. Believing he'd be transported into the magical-mystical world of meditation, with water drops, calming music and maybe even some 4D incense stuff, he was surprised to land on a website that was far from fancy. The references, however, were more than impressive, including athletes, actors, politicians, and business leaders. "Ling's the man!" Peter told the monitor, excitedly. The monitor didn't reply.

Peter searches the site and found: Contact Us. "I have to talk to this guy," Peter thought, "Even if it's just to make this website better! Let's see where he works. Probably 4800 miles away in Tibet, I suspect." To Peter's surprise, Ling Ho - Meditation Master was less than 100 miles south, in a nearby city. Peter was confident that Ling Ho was definitely what he needed, so he filled in the online form and hit 'submit'.

Chapter Four – Meeting Ling Ho

After several weeks of interruptions and more than ten emails, Ling Ho agreed to meet. It was a Tuesday and the rains was pounding down. Peter's work schedule had absolutely exploded and every excuse known to man had popped up to stop him from making the 83-mile drive.

But Peter had sought out Ling and he was fully determined to make the meeting. Nothing was going to stop him. He wanted answers and needed them more than ever. He didn't have time to read 15 books. Truth be known, he didn't have time to read one book! Tim was pressuring him to invest more money to keep things flowing but Peter wanted a change before another nickel was invested. Eventually time would prevail and the decision would be made for both of them. He knew that in business, when decisions need to be made, procrastination is the killer of dreams. With coffee in hand, iPhone fully charged, and voicemail changed, Peter got into his car and made his way to Ling Ho's.

The rain was intense. The phone was buzzing, dinging and pinging every two minutes. Peter wondered what was going on. His staff was usually great at operating without him, but today, an outside force seemed to be trying to stop him from meeting Ling Ho. It took Peter a strenuous three and a half hours to drive a mere 83 miles, but finally he arrived at 2916 Coldwell Ave East.

He entered the building, looking for Unit 625. "Of course, there's no elevator. Why would there be?" Peter sighed in frustration. There were stairs. Narrow, steep stairs. He slouched, looked down and began to climb the six flights. Not six regular flights. To Peter, they felt like double flights. "What kind of building is this? I feel like I've been on a stair-climber for a half hour!" Finally, he reached the sixth floor and saw Unit 625. A sign on the door read: Ling HO-MEDITATION MASTER. "This is it," said Peter and headed in.

Ling Ho's offices were very modest. A simple mahogany reception desk sat unattended with a small sign reading: "Ring bell or wait until we sense you are here." The paintings on the wall were the black velvet kind that reminded Peter of his childhood and the countless hours spent colouring the horses and the race cars. There were two chairs on the right, church basement style. Adorning the corner was a small table with candles, herbs and crystals. Peter's eyebrows lifted as he began to become suspicious that he might just have seen the extent of their retail sales. On the far left wall were photos of an unassuming man standing shoulder to shoulder with North America's power elite. Ling Ho's image was not what Peter expected. He'd anticipated a powerful, easily recognizable figure who wouldn't be forgotten, but Ling would easily be missed in a crowd of four. He was a small, slight man with unremarkable, regular features. Nothing stood out except one thing - the look on his face in each picture. Though decades had passed between the first and last photos, and more grey hair had been added, his demeanour was unchanged... he was calm.

Peter rang the bell softly, just touching the top with his finger and quickly stopping the sound with his other hand.

'Don't disrupt the calm.' Peter thought. Standing nervously at the front with a goofy look on his face he patiently waited for the great man to appear. He was anxious for Ling Ho to give him the answers and send him home to save the day.

Nothing.

"He must not have heard me," thought Peter, deciding to ring the bell again. This time, he accidentally smacked the bell with a force that would have made a Viking proud. The sound echoed through the room, loud enough to cut concrete.

"Yikes! What have I done?" Peter's nervousness intensified as he flashed back to days spent outside the principal's office.

"Breathe." he said in a low voice. "Just breathe."

Ling Ho walked in. "Did you feel the bell needed punishment for its feeble first ring?"

The look on his face was rock solid. Peter had spent decades reading the poker faces of people selling their businesses, but he could tell, this guy was serious.

"No. I'm sorry," said Peter. "I hope I didn't break it."

"Don't say sorry to me. I'm not the bell." Said Ling Ho, with a bit of a smile. "Welcome, Mr. Strikman. Please. Come. Sit." He gestured down the hall to a small sitting area with three chairs.

Sitting down, Peter welcomed the warm softness. The chair pulled him in as though he was no longer in control. The three-hour drive had taken its toll and his heart was racing. On the small table were three glasses of water, three tea cups, and a plate with three cookies.

"Would you like some tea?" Ling Ho asked.

"That would be great, thank you." Peter replied.

Ling Ho filled all three tea cups.

Peter wondered who else was joining them. Was some spirit sitting next to them? Was Ling a freak who thought he had an imaginary friend? Peter's mind jerked back into overdrive.

Ling Ho paused and looked Peter directly in the eyes, as if waiting for him to finish the thought. Startled, Peter wondered: 'Did I say that out loud?!'

Charging ahead, Peter said, "Mr. Ho, thank you for meeting me today. I really appreciate it."

"Please, call me Ling," said Ling Ho.

"Okay Ling, I think I understand what you do, but I was wondering if we could go over it one more time."

"Sure, Peter," said Ling. "Clarity is paramount. My role is simple; I teach you to still your mind and you pay me." The pause was long, and his face was firm. "My fee is $10,000. You pay $2,500 today, $2,500 when we are done and the remaining $5,000 when you feel you have benefitted from the teachings."

"That's what I thought. I understand, thanks Ling. Do you want the payment now?" Peter asked.

"No, you can wait until the end of today's session. Let's be sure you are still wanting this when the hour is complete," said Ling. "What you do with the teachings is up to you. What you discover is based on how much you want to hear. What you decide to block out is for you to deal with." With that statement, Ling paused for a moment and continued without blinking an eye. "The journey is a simple one for me and as complex for you as you decide it to be."

Peter replied quickly, “Simple works for me, Ling. You know my situation. I need to shut down the outside noise so I can focus on what needs to get done. Help me still my mind. Please.”

“Very well,” Ling said, gesturing to Peter to get up. He pointed behind Peter with his hand.

Peter looked over his shoulder and tried to get out of the chair. His back was tight and the softness of the chair had sucked him in. Breaking free of the grip, he stood up and started down the hall.

Ling walked softly. Peter followed, thinking: “Here goes.”

Door after door, room after room, the short hallway seemed to stretch forever. They stopped at the second last door, and Ling opened it, gesturing for them to enter. Peter stopped abruptly at the threshold, thrown by what he saw. The room was tiny - only six feet wide and 10 feet long - making it more of a closet than a room. White walls, blue-green carpet. A window at one end with a roller blind overlooked two chairs. Two church-basement chrome and blue vinyl chairs. No pictures, no desk, no little Buddha in the corner. Nothing but two chairs.

Peter, realizing he was still standing at the threshold, gave his head a quick shake and walked in. His blood pressure jumped a notch and his face was on fire.

Ling followed, and Peter swore he was smiling.

“Sit, please” said Ling. Peter chose the first chair, which put the window to the left and the door to the right.

Ling sat in the other chair facing him - their knees were nearly touching.

Peter was completely on edge, not knowing whether to run, laugh, or buckle down and deal with the situation.

He chose to stay.

Chapter Five – Meditation 101

The two men sat, not moving. Ling's eyes were shut. Peter looked around like a nervous school boy at a Grade 8 dance, wondering what to do. Finally he too closed his eyes and, like a light switch, his brain hit full speed, or so he thought. Questions appeared faster than he could answer them.

'What am I doing here?'

'Who is this quack?'

'What kind of idiot drives 83 miles in the pouring rain to sit in a church-basement chair, knee to knee with a 2,000 year old Asian man who'd freak out the calmest of people?'

'Is he looking at me?'

'Does he still have his eyes closed?'

'Am I being pranked?'

Finally Ling spoke, "Breathe, Peter."

Peter inhaled deeply then let the breath go.

"You have a busy mind." Ling stated as if he'd heard every thought.

"Yah, I guess so, Ling," Peter replied, opening his eyes.

Ling looked into Peter's eyes, and deep into his soul. The comfort Peter saw in Ling's eyes soothed his tension so completely he was almost physically drawn in and struggled to stay on the chair.

Ling's eyes remained locked on Peter's. Unflinching, soft, counselling eyes.

Slowly, a small smile appeared on Ling's face and his eyes softened even more.

"It's okay, Peter. Why have you come here?" Ling wasn't looking for an answer. "Do you think you will actually reply to your own questions?"

Ling let his question hang in the air like thick syrup.

Peter contemplated the question "Do I think I will reply?" he asked.

Ling saw he'd broken through to Peter and his smile grew. He decided to ease Peter's bewilderment.

"The questions you asked yourself were great questions. They were real, they were pure and they were deserving of answers. Those answers came as fast as your questions and you knew that. Why do you think you asked so many things, in so many ways?" Link asked. "Your mind was closed to the answers. The questions were always there, Peter, and so were the answers. The question really is... can you slow down, hear the answers and most importantly, not judge them?"

Before Peter could begin to think of a response, Ling moved on.

"Okay, close your eyes." Ling said. "We're going to help you to slow that mighty brain of yours, but first we'll work to have you in the room with me."

Peter opened his eyes wide, thinking wildly: 'Say what?!'

"Close your eyes Peter," said Ling. "You are physically here, we both know that. Now I need you mentally and spiritually here. First let's 'center' your thoughts. Take a few deep breaths in and out. It's all about being relaxed, Peter. There are 1000s of ways to meditate. I am not here to teach you the 'one and only right' way, just 'a' way. So let's begin. Imagine a ball of light in front of you, about the size of a golf ball. A bright light. Do you see it?" Ling stopped, waiting for Peter to answer.

"Umm? Sure." Peter replied simply to keep the lesson moving. He thought he saw a golf ball, but didn't want to say so.

"Great," said Ling. "Now move that ball into the center of your heart. Bring it slowly through your chest and into your heart. A bright light smack dab in the middle of your heart. Are you focused on that?" he asked.

Peter nodded but found he had a golf *club* in his mind - not a bright light. Trying to shake the 9-iron image, he worked hard to see a light.

"Okay, now we need to make sure you are also grounded." Ling said. "Imagine a cable or cord connecting you to the center of the earth. It's connected to the base of your spine straight down to the center of the earth. Hook it in. Feel it hold you in the chair like a tether."

Peter strapped a steel cable in his mind and smiled slightly at this freaky old guy trying to teach him, the president of the company, to connect to the planet.

"Now imagine something flowing along that cable from the base of your spine to the earth." Ling saw his student's eyebrows scrunch as he tried to see this 'flow'. "Don't judge it Peter. It is what it is. Sometimes it will be a waterfall, sometimes syrup, sometimes thin, sometimes huge. See what you see and don't judge it. Now let's ask those questions again."

Peter smiled as he though back to what those questions were, but questioned whether Ling seriously wanted him to say them out loud.

"Do you want me to say them out loud?" Peter finally asked.

"Do you want to say them out loud?" Ling replied.

"I don't know," was all Peter could say.

"Well, if you don't know what you want, I surely don't. Focus on the ball of light and the flowing cord." He paused. "Do you want to say them out loud?"

"No."

"Okay."

They sat in silence for what seemed forever. Peter finally broke the silence, "What I want to know is why I'm here."

"And your answer is?" Ling states.

"To get the answers."

"Very good. You just got one."

Peter was a bit frustrated with that reply, but understood that Ling was technically right. Not exactly what Peter wanted to hear, but Ling was right. Peter continued to think the guy was a freak.

"Breathe Peter." Ling cut in. "In and out. Feel the comfort of being grounded and centered."

They sat quietly for a few more minutes.

"Now open your eyes when you are ready." Ling said softly.

Peter opened his eyes and saw Ling staring at him, smiling.

"The hour is complete." Ling said.

"Really?" Peter asked, astonished.

"Really." Ling stated, with a slight smile in his voice.

Within seconds, Ling left the room and Peter followed. Ling stepped behind the reception desk, looking Peter right in the eyes. Without a word spoken, the check book came out and a $2,500 check was written. In one move Peter had embarked on a journey that he felt he might soon regret. Goodbyes were said, and Peter returned to his car and headed back to the office.

Later that evening when he got home and realized what had happened, he took out the new notepad he'd been given to take notes during the hour. He wrote down everything he'd learned. His brain was trying to encapsulate what he'd experienced. Not much, he thought as he struggled to justify paying Ling's astronomical fee.

"This better be worth it."

Ling HO – MEDITATION

MASTER TEACHINGS

- See ball of light and move into center of heart.
- Connect cord from butt to earth.

Chapter Six – Reading People

Seven days had passed since Peter and Ling met. Tim had continued to add stress to Peter's life. No decisions had been made since their last meeting and though they hadn't been in the same room since, emails had been flying and none were moving them forward. Peter's brain had never been busier and he was painfully aware that while he had no idea what Ling had taught him, he knew was $2,500 poorer. Each morning and then as each email arrived, Peter tried to focus on that golf ball of light. It seemed more like a flashlight with dying batteries. Frustrated, he thought: 'I can't keep my focus on anything other than being frustrated by all the questions.'

But because Peter had always been a man who finished what he committed to, he found himself back in the car, once again going to meet Ling. This time the meeting point was closer to Peter's office. 'He probably feels guilty for taking $2,500 and sitting me on a chair in that tin can of a room.' Thought Peter as he pushed the start button and turned the dial to D.

The meeting time was 1:23 pm - weird. "1:23? What kind of a time is that to meet?" Peter said out loud as he drove. "What's he going to do today? Stare at me for another hour?" Condescendingly Peter repeated Ling's words: "'Very good. You just got an answer.' That's all I got from last week. That's it? 'You got an answer.' What am I doing? I'm $2,500 down, that's bad enough, but now I'm going to waste another hour? This is stupi..."

Screech!

Peter locked the brakes as hard as he could. The car in front of him had suddenly stopped.

"Look out!" Peter yelled while his heart kicked into full gear, the adrenalin shooting through his body like a bolt of lightning. Preparing for impact, all of Peter's systems switched on. His arms stiffened, his left leg braced while his right pushed even harder on the brake, his face contorted into a locked scream and his eyes closed tightly.

Screech.

And then...nothing. Peter braced for the smash. The crumple of steel, the cracking of plastic, the explosion of the air bag. But there was nothing.

He opened his eyes. He was so close to the car in front of him that he could read their dashboard.

"What are you doing you moron, you idiot?" Peter screamed at the top of his lungs before realizing they were stopped at a red light.

'How did I miss that?' he wondered.

Fully awake and in the moment, Peter was grateful that his car windows were closed. His psychotic yelling had been reserved just for him. The light turned green and Peter sheepishly drove on, to meet Ling.

Pulling into the parkade, he found a spot, shut the car off and took a few minutes to breathe.

"Maybe I need Ling more than I think," said Peter realizing he really might have to relearn the art of focussing.

The meeting was set for Arista's Coffee in the Sunshine Mall - a small gathering hole known for its great coffee. It was Peter's choice as Ling had asked for a place with people and Arista's offered great private tables for talking.

Peter looked at his watch as he walked through the door of the coffee shop. 1:25 pm, he was two minutes late and he hated being late. He quickly searched for Ling, and found him sitting in a quiet corner sipping a drink.

“Hello Ling. Sorry I’m late.” Peter said, striding briskly, hand outstretched in greeting.

“That’s twice you have been sorry. You did me no harm,” said Ling, shaking Peter’s hand. “Grab a drink, and we will talk when you are settled.”

Peter stood in line. The girl at the counter was busy punching keys, trying to keep up with the constant barrage of customer requests. The barista beside her was calmly filling orders, mechanically placing completed drinks on the bar and yelling the full version of the code on the cup. Finally Peter’s was ready and he went back to the table. Ling was gone. Peter looked around and found Ling standing by the doors to the mall, smiling his freaky smile.

“Where are we heading?” Peter asked.

“Lesson #2.” Ling replied.

All Peter could think was ‘I don’t even understand Lesson #1! Was that really a lesson? What am I in for now?’

“There are ten basic lessons. Ten steps to clarity if you will.” Ling continued, “These 10 steps are merely the beginning, I am sorry to say, but they will give you the clarity you initially seek. As I stated when we first met, meditation is something that changes with you as you journey. My role is to open your mind and still the noise.”

“Okay” Peter agreed. “Bring on lesson 2.” Feeling fully awake and empowered, the near accident had definitely woken him up. He was ready and willing to learn.

“Follow me.” Ling walked down the mall. Peter was feeling a bit awkward, thinking that everyone was watching them. Peter stood more than six feet tall in his $2,000 Italian suit while Ling on a good day was five feet tall and was wearing an old T-shirt and linen pants. They stood out from the crowd.

Ling went to the center of the mall and parked himself on one of the couches. Peter joined him like the seasoned shopping-husband he is, as he had spent many hours sitting on couches with Sam, waiting for Marie and Jessica.

Peter looked at Ling who had his eyes closed and was sitting peacefully. Peter looked around thinking to himself, ‘Well if we didn’t stand out before, we sure do now.’

Ling opened his eyes, staring right at Peter.

“Okay Peter. Time to do the golf ball thing.”

“Here?”

“Yes, here.”

“Really?”

“Yes, really.”

“Open or closed?”

“What do you think?”

“Fine, whatever you say Ling.”

Ling continued softly and confidently as if he were the only person in the building. “Imagine a golf ball of light, Peter. It is a bright light. Close your eyes. Imagine that ball of light out in front of you. Move it into the center of your heart. Got it?”

“Sort of.”

“Focus on it.”

‘Not really bright, but it’s there, I guess.”

“Great, Peter, now it’s time to ground. Remember that cable I spoke of last week? Imagine it connected from the base of your spine to the center of the earth. Hook in the cable. Ground yourself.”

“Okay.”

“Make sure it is flowing. See the flow. Do not judge it, just make sure it is flowing down your grounding cord.”

“Done.”

Purposefully Ling said, “Now slowly open your eyes, but keep the ball of light there as well as your grounding cord.”

Peter cautiously opened his eyes, fully expecting people to be pointing and laughing. But no one had even noticed them. They were just two guys hanging out on the couch.

Ling began a one-way conversation. “The first thing you need to believe, Peter, is that you already know everything I am going to teach you.” The lesson had clearly begun. “You hold within you all the power you need in order to focus, all the strength to make decisions and all the clarity to understand the consequences.” Ling was speaking in a calm and methodical voice, articulating clearly. “Everything you will experience, you have already experienced. The talents you have already tapped into to build your companies have been in you all along. Within you, Peter, lies great, great power."

Peter felt his back straighten and his chest rise. Lesson Two already felt better than Lesson One. All other sounds of the mall faded and Peter heard only Ling's voice. Though people walked by every second, Peter focused only on Ling's words.

Ling continued, "You have always been able to understand people, assess their purpose, predict their motives and either lead them to their goals or show them there is a better path."

'How does he know this?' Peter asked himself. 'Maybe that's not hard to predict, I guess anyone in my position would fit that description.'

"Today," Ling said, pausing, "we start to show you this."

With those words Peter began to feel whoozy as the excitement grew. He felt like a little kid who'd just been told he was about to meet Santa.

"Be sure you still can see the ball of light and the grounding cord. Do you still have them?" Ling asked.

"I think so."

"Close your eyes if you must, but make sure they are there."

"Okay. Got them."

"Great. Now look around you. What do you see?"

"Capitalism." Peter said with a smile, but Ling didn't react or reply. "I see several stores. GAP, HMV, Sony, Build-a-Bear, Old Navy. I see people shopping, buying, complaining. I see kids working the tills.

Some standing around doing nothing, some smiling and helping customers. Is that what you mean?"

Ling didn't reply so Peter continued. "I see people walking from store to store. I see people strolling around and I see people hustling through.

"I see you." Peter said with another smile, completely baffled by what he was supposed to do.

"Look Peter. Look deep. Don't just see. L O O K," Ling said slowly and purposefully as he gestured at a point in the distance.

Peter paused, took a good look around and said, "I see 30 foot ceilings with glass panels. Each panel is at the perfect angle to make pyramids the entire length of the mall. I see advertisements on banners hung every 100 feet or so. I see cables strewn across the mall, I suspect for seasonal decorations. I see cameras on the walls. I see an office way at the top. Hmph. I've never noticed any of that before."

"What else?" Ling asked.

"Okay, I see three girls, about 16 years old, giggling. The blonde on the left is clearly the leader. Her walk is more confident. The girl in brown in the middle seems lost, looking around constantly. Her friends appear to be protecting her. She feels secure in the middle.

"The shorter girl on the right seems shy. She has the most shopping bags, but carries herself less confidently. Her clothes say she fits in, but her body-language says otherwise."

The girls' eyes met Peter's and though they were oblivious, he instantly felt like a creeper, as Jessica called it, and he quickly looked at Ling.

Ling knew he had to say something to keep Peter in the moment. "Very good, Peter. You looked. What else do you see?"

"I see a boyfriend reluctantly shopping with his girlfriend. They are at the tills now and he is reaching into his pocket to pay. Her instant affection after she spots the wallet is his reward. It appears to make her happy. They are heading to the next store. Her giddy walk and clutching arms exemplify her excitement."

Peter couldn't help feeling sorry for the boy. Like a fly to a bright light, the girl dragged her boy across the mall. His excitement was completely gone and a new bar had been set for him... shoes.

"From the look on his face I suspect he has neither the courage nor the heart to say no, nor does he have the money to say yes. Certain disappointment for someone is on its way."

"Very good, Peter," Ling said. "The mom there with her two kids, what do you see? Go beyond the obvious. Look more deeply, Peter."

"She's tired." Peter said, unable to find any other words.

"Of?" Ling asked.

"Life." Peter was fully focused on the woman and the kids.

"Stay grounded Peter, and remember the cord." Ling cut through the silence.

"I can't describe it. That's all that I can think of," he said.

"Notice," said Ling, "Notice what you see. Say the words as they come to mind."

"Tired. Stressed. Unhappy." Words came from Peter's lips but his mind generated many more and he paused to collect them. "She doesn't want to be here. Her grip on her son's arm is stronger than she wants it to be, but she's tired of his antics. She has a wedding band on so I suspect she's married. The pile of bags in the stroller says she has been here a while. Not one of the bags is from a women's store. Maybe she resents that. Who knows?"

"What do you know Peter?" Ling asked.

"I know only what I see." Peter replied.

"That's not necessarily true, Peter, Ling said calmly. "What you're doing right now, in essence, is reading her energy but what you may pick up is a mirror image of who you are. We see whatever we notice and we notice what we are willing to look at, describe and not judge. That is the hardest thing to learn, Peter. Don't judge her, just notice. As you look around, try not to judge anything. Just notice, and describe, and then be aware of how it makes you feel inside."

With the slowness and gentleness of a true master, Ling asked, "What feelings does seeing the woman bring up?"

"Sadness." Peter said the first word that came to mind.

"Where do you feel it on your body, Peter?"

"Chest, I guess... and throat."

"Okay. Acknowledge that. Remember it and let's move on."

The two men continued to watch people for the remainder of the hour and what Peter 'noticed' seemed to intensify - everything from the nervous trainee at Old Navy, to the mall walkers who walk past every 7.5 minutes.

"Time is up, Peter," said Ling after Peter described the man asleep on the couch beside them. "What did you 'notice'?"

“Everything,” said Peter, proud as a peacock. “I saw things that I’ve never seen before and I have been here many times. I am...”

“That’s true.” Ling stopped Peter in mid-sentence. “You are. You are part of what is happening right here. This is what it is like to truly ‘be’ in a moment. You were focused purely on one thing at a time. What you saw is what you described. Your eyes and ears saw and heard much more but you focused on one thing at a time for an hour. You have in you the power to focus and, as no surprise to me, a great ability to read a situation. I suspect you know that though, don’t you?”

“I guess I forgot. This was fun, Ling, thanks.”

“I did nothing. You did everything.”

“Thank you anyway, Ling.”

The two of them parted ways and Peter was pleased that Lesson Two had been much better than Lesson One. At the end of the day, he continued his notes. Sitting on his deck, sipping a glass of wine, he wrote down what he had learned so far.

Ling HO – MEDITATION

MASTER TEACHINGS

Lesson One

- See ball of light and move into center of heart.
- Connect cord from butt to earth.

Lesson Two

- Do lesson one over again.
- Focus on what is behind what you see.
- Block other things out and notice.
- Watch how people act and hear the words that come to mind.
- Be attuned to where on your body you feel something when the descriptors come up.
- Do <u>NOT</u> judge (very hard).
- Be aware that many things are happening at the same time.
- BE IN THE MOMENT.

Chapter Seven – Gut Feeling

"How was the week?" Ling asked.

"Not bad actually Ling, thanks for asking." Peter replied.

"Still judging things I see!" Ling said with a huge smile.

Peter laughed and clarified, "It was very productive. I used some of the techniques you taught me."

Peter's week had been productive. Much was due to Tim not being there hence causing the team to sense less stress in the office. Reality was still reality, but Peter felt he could better see the bigger picture and focus on the forward-and-out, rather than the in-and-back - something he hadn't done for months. "A couple times I really couldn't get the ball of light to appear, but all-in-all, my focus was better. Can I say 'better'?"

"You can say anything you want."

"True enough." Peter smiled.

"Okay Peter, are you ready for today's lesson?"

"Yes, I am, Ling. Yes, I am."

"Have you ever heard of chakras?" Ling asked.

"I've heard the term, but have absolutely no idea what they are." Peter's honesty with Ling was improving. He remembered seeing chakras mentioned in nearly every book he picked up at the book store, but he didn't have the patience then - nor did he feel he had now - to understand his chakras.

"How about auras?"

Peter flinched and prepared himself for the weird stuff. Auras, chakras, yeesh. He was clearly uncomfortable.

As usual Ling seemed to hear Peter's thoughts or perhaps he saw the look of sheer fear and he quickly said, "Don't worry, Peter, I'm not going to freak you out. No 'weirdo stuff' as you'd call it. I know what your objective is and I'm just giving you the basics so you can clear your mind."

"Thanks, Ling."

"You are welcome. So I take it 'No' is the answer to my aura question?"

Peter nodded with a sheepish smile.

"Today we are going to learn what 'feeling it in the pit of your stomach' really means." Ling started on one of his don't-interrupt-me talks. "We all have those thoughts: 'I've got a bad feeling about this', 'my stomach doesn't feel good', 'I have a lump in my throat' ... Ever say those things, Peter?"

"Sure, everyone does."

"Let's go into meditation and talk about what they mean. Close your eyes. Imagine a ball of light, Peter. It is a bright light. Imagine that ball of light out in front of you. Move it into the center of your heart. When you have that, imagine your grounding cord. A cord connected from the base of your spine to the center of the earth. Hook in the cable. Ground yourself. Make sure it is flowing. See the flow. Do not judge it, just make sure it is flowing down your grounding cord." Ling's routine was clear.

"Got it."

"Good," Ling started, "Everything has energy and energy is constantly flowing. I'm sure you have heard that before Peter, so that's probably not new. Your personal energy though is very, very important. It is a combination of the energy coming from the earth mixed with energy from the universe and energy from the Source. This energy flows through you and creates an energy field around your body."

Peter heard the words and lost focus. 'A wha?? Did I hear him right? Energy field?'

"Stay focused," said Ling. "This energy is your energy. Take time to visualize it encompassing your body – it surrounds your body approximately an arm's length all around."

"Okay..." Peter replied sceptically.

"This is what is called your aura. It is like your 'personal' space. This distance around your body is for you. It is *your* space." Ling continued to ignore Peter's scepticism. "The size determines greatly how you are feeling at this moment, large and you are seeking control or spreading yourself too thin. Small and you are not willing to share or are vulnerable. Try to keep it an arm's length around your body as that is a manageable size. Regardless of size, auras can always use a refresh. As people come into your space at work or at home, they leave a mark - like the feeling you get when someone is just too close to you. They may be trying to tap into your energy." Ling drove home his point.

"I've felt that," Peter replied as he drifted off to memories of partners, customers, staff members all looking to him for energy when times got tough.

"Okay," Ling settled in as he suspected Peter was finally getting the concept. "So, what we're going to do is clean your space. Are you ready?"

"I don't like cleaning much Ling, but sure," Peter said, trying to be witty.

"This cleaning feels good...most of the time." Ling laughed a 'I-know-something-you-don't' laugh. "Not only is there cleaning that needs to be done, but sometimes recharging is needed. This 'space' or 'aura' flows just like your grounding cord. What we want to do is just go with the flow. The energy is flowing from above your head down to below your feet and down your grounding cord."

Peter opened his eyes to see if Ling was demonstrating. Ling was sitting perfectly still, back straight, palms up, with a purely peaceful, joyful look on his face. Peter yearned for that feeling.

Ling continued, "With your mind, help that flow move along. Try to speed it up. Look for spots that are not moving."

"I'm not sure I'm getting this, Ling."

"You will," Ling replied. "Just focus on it. There is no right or wrong, just whatever comes to your mind, work with it."

"I'll try."

"Good. Look for any black spots, especially behind you. Comb through them helping the 'flow', clean that stuff away. People love to leave their crap in here for you to deal with. Remember it is their crap, not yours. Move it out of your space. Envision white light energy taking over those dark areas - recharging and cleansing, taking your energy back."

With that Peter fully increased his concentration. He lived and breathed people leaving their crap with him – that was a daily ritual!

"Very good, Peter," Ling says.

Those words rocked Peter as he couldn't understand what Ling was seeing that prompted him to say "Very good." He realized Ling was seeing the determination on his face.

"Just relax. Breathe in and out. Focus on recharging your energy." Ling cut through again. Peter absorbed the calmness in Ling's voice. Ling let those instructions hang in the air while Peter focused on cleaning the crap out. "Okay Peter, when you're ready, open your eyes and come out of meditation." He waited calmly for Peter's eyes to focus on him before continuing, "That's your aura. You can clean that any time you want. It's your space. You look as though you're enjoying this, so feel free to do this cleaning whenever you want."

Peter chuckled, "Guess I'm tired of others leaving their stuff."

"Soon you will be at a spot where they can't 'leave their stuff' unless you want it. Truth be known, you have been allowing all that stuff to be left there. But that's another lesson."

"Great." Peter said sarcastically.

"While you have that clean aura of yours flowing, let's run the chakras," said Ling.

Peter raised an eyebrow then quickly lowered it, hoping that Ling hadn't seen.

"We're going to help you understand why you feel reactions in certain parts of your body. 'Gut feeling', 'pain in chest', etc."

Both of Peter's eyebrows lifted, but this time in excitement. He followed his gut often, but never really knew why.

"Let's go back into meditation. Close your eyes. Imagine a ball of light Peter. It is a bright light. Imagine that ball of light out in front of you. Move it into the center of your heart. When you have that, imagine your grounding cord. A cord connected from the base of your spine to the center of the earth. Hook in the cable. Ground yourself. Make sure it is flowing. See the flow. Do not judge it, just make sure it is flowing down your grounding cord." Giving Peter a few minutes, Ling waited then said, "So Peter, when you have a gut feeling, where do you feel it?"

"Stomach, solar plexus area." Peter calmly replied.

"Okay, that is what is known as your third chakra, a 'state of power', 'control', 'self-esteem'. It's where you feel your purpose and hence your gut feeling." Ling stated. "Now what about that mother in the mall? Where did you feel something? Do you remember?"

Peter pretended to think hard, but the answer has been burned into his memory. "Chest and throat." he replied.

"Those my friend are your fourth and fifth chakras kicking in. Chest is fourth - 'unconditional love', 'love of others', 'love of self' and the throat is your fifth - 'speech', 'communication', 'clarity of words' 'stating your intentions to the world'."

"So why did that woman make my chest and throat ache?" Peter asked.

"Good question."

"I don't love her, I don't even know her."

"Or do you?"

"What?" Peter's eyes opened in shock.

"Just kidding Peter, that's Lesson 43," Ling laughed.

Peter closed his eyes again and tried to find that ball of light.

"What you feel when you assess or read a situation has as much to do with you as it does with the thing or person you are seeing."

"So it's like a mirror?" Peter asked.

"Yes, sort of. Let's take the woman...you felt a tightness in your chest and had a lump in your throat, correct?"

"Yes."

"What in your life, current or past, does she reflect?"

Peter was shocked at the question as he had never really thought about that. "She was probably a good reflection of how my wife, Marie, felt when I worked a billion hours a week and she had to do everything with the family."

"Good. And do you have those feelings again right now?"

"Umm? Yes."

"Good. So let's clean that out so you can move on as obviously it is still lingering with you."

"No doubt."

"Cleaning chakras is something I can't teach you in 10 weeks, but essentially a chakra is energy going from the front of your body through the body, out the back and down your grounding."

Peter's threshold for understanding hit a max. 'Huh?' was all his brain could do with that information.

"Don't worry too much about that. What we want to do is acknowledge the feeling you are having, understand what you need to do to have closure and then push the feeling out the back, down and away. Focus on your throat Peter; that lump in your throat." Ling continues, "What do you think that means?"

Peter thought for a while, because he often got that feeling. "That I want to say something?" he finally said.

"Like what?"

"I don't know."

"Try."

"I wanted to tell her that life gets better, kids get older. Time to do things for yourself eventually comes."

"Anything else?"

"Sorry." Peter said with absolute shame. "I wanted to say sorry to my wife for not appreciating, not seeing what she was experiencing."

Silence held the room for a few minutes.

"You just cleared your fifth Peter." Ling said with pride in his voice. "Those feelings appear when we 'notice' something. When we take the time to look at the feeling, we can understand it, and when we understand it, we can move it along, deal with it or act upon it."

"Cool, I get this." Peter replied with excitement. "You said there are seven chakras. What are the other four?"

Ling, knowing he had Peter's attention, began his education. "Your first chakra is down by your testicles and it is 'security' – 'survival in body, finances and life', 'Can we make payroll?', etc. Second is by your lower abdomen and is related to 'emotions' as well as 'sexuality' and 'sensuality'. Third is your solar plexus as we mentioned, fourth is your heart, fifth is your throat and sixth is on your forehead and that is 'clairvoyance'. That's one you'll probably focus on a lot." Ling looked Peter right between the eyes. "The seventh is on the top of your head and it is a 'state of consciousness of enlightenment', sometimes called 'knowingness'. Many will try to tap into your knowledge. Do you get headaches often?" Ling asked.

"Sometimes, yes. Doozies." Peter answered with a slight question in his voice.

"Usually that is a sign you are trying to do too much with your knowingness, either by training or being brain-drained unwillingly."

"Ya, I do that one a lot." Peter said. "But that's what is expected of a leader."

Ling paused then stated, "Could be, but I believe a leader is one who selects the way to go and helps people find their inner power to be a part of the journey. That to me is a leader, rather than one who knows everything and just needs people to do what they are told."

With that Ling drove home a knockout punch of information. Peter knew it all, but Ling had the uncanny ability to tell him what he had forgotten or taken for granted. 'Which leader am I?' Peter asked himself.

"You are questioning yourself, Peter?" Ling asked just as Peter's mind finished the question. Peter was starting to hate the guy.

"Just thinking Ling," Peter replied.

"Why are you doing that?" Ling asked slowly.

"You posed a good question."

“Did I?” Ling asked. “I don’t think I asked a question.”

Again he opened Peter up to question himself. ‘Didn’t he? I’m sure he asked me a question. No, he just stated his belief and I created the question. Now my head hurts!’

“Nice and easy Peter.” Ling said with the greatest softness. “No need to think so hard. It is in the thinking, that we forget to feel. Feeling and clarity are synonymous. Once you know an answer, act on it. Sometimes ‘thinking’ confuses the answer and begins to justify inaction. Then you forget to just be, feel and act.” Ling continued, “Energy is always flowing, everywhere. You can only control your own energy. Remember that trying to control others is an act of futility and is not in the highest integrity of the universe.”

Peter, being well versed in this, said confidently, “Circle of influence, circle of control. I get it, Ling.”

“Yes, but in the world of meditation, your only circle of control is your aura. Your personal space. You can control that. That is all. And once you can control your own personal space, you can start to block out all the noise and truly find the answer you seek.” Ling concluded with an absolute hard stop. This lesson was obviously at an end.

Ling HO – MEDITATION

MASTER TEACHINGS

Lesson One

- See ball of light and move into center of heart.
- Connect cord from butt to earth.

Lesson Two

- Do lesson one over again.
- Focus on what is behind what you see.
- Block other things out and notice.
- Watch how people act and hear the words that come to mind.
- Be attuned to where on your body you feel something when the descriptors come up.
- Do <u>NOT</u> judge (very hard).
- Be aware that many things are happening at the same time as you are happening.

BE IN THE MOMENT

Lesson Three – CHAKRAS

Big lesson today! Gut feeling, headaches, control.

- Your personal space is the only circle of control.
- The personal space (aka aura) surrounds body like an energy field approximately an arm's length around body.

- Energy flows up from ground, down from universe.
- My personal energy flows around me and through my "CHAKRAS".
- 7 Chakras
  - 1st – privates - survival
  - 2nd – belly button - emotions & sensuality/sexuality
  - 3rd - solar plexus – gut feeling, purpose, control
  - 4th – heart – love for others & self
  - 5th – throat – communication
  - 6th – forehead – clairvoyance
  - 7th – top of head – knowingness, enlightenment

- When I feel something like a lump in my throat, I first acknowledge the feeling, try to understand it and then move it through my body and down my grounding. *ASK Ling MORE*
- Thinking can lead to justifying. True answer is usually in first feeling.
- When I control my space and clear everything out I will then be able to find the answer.

Chapter Eight – Get Out of My Space.

Peter had a meeting scheduled with Tim to continue their discussion of what to do next. For a few days Peter had been trying everything Ling taught him. In some cases it seemed to be working but in others, not so much. Peter found he was trying to own his space but the real challenge would be in the first few minutes after Tim arrived.

"Peter, I haven't heard a word from you in days, is that any way to treat a partner?" Tim said coldly before any hellos or handshakes – neither of which happened at that meeting and might never happen again.

"Just running the business, Tim. There was nothing I needed from you and we're just trying to make it through." Peter was practicing noticing what came up while replying to Tim's harsh comments. Everything seemed to be on fire though so it was difficult to determine which part of his body he was feeling at any given moment.

"So you have decided to keep going...good." Tim said feeling as if he'd won Peter over to his side.

"Actually, no, Tim, I haven't decided that." Peter didn't bite on Tim's words. He flowed the words away, not allowing them into his space.

"So what did you decide?" Tim asked.

"Nothing." Peter said passively.

"I thought you were that 'Meetings are for decisions' guy who said we had to make a decision and get going." Tim threw Peter's words from discussions of the past back into his face.

"But I don't have a different answer than I did before." Peter tried with all his might not to bite. His first and third chakras lit up but he didn't notice.

Tim quickly retorted, "And I told you that answer won't work. You can't operate this company with fewer people. You won't survive. My retirement fund rests on the survival of this company and if we have to invest another $100,000 to save it, we will. You're young enough to do this again, but I can't. If I invest the money will I get it back?" Tim's anger and pleading were in conflict.

"Not unless we fix the problem." Peter said slowly and methodically. He had said those words so many times in the past that he knew they wouldn't matter. Tim had no desire to downsize the organization to match the sales and felt the only solution was to sell more even though sales had already been increased.

"So how are you going to fix it? What's your plan?" Tim's anger prevailed over the pleading.

"Seriously? What's my plan?" Peter had lost all control, was no longer feeling his chakras or his aura and had lost every bit of patience. He was completely oblivious to his surroundings and couldn't have read the energy had it been in 3D colour in front of his face. Tim had just jumped into Peter's personal space.

Peter blurted: "If in your great wisdom, we can't run the organization with fewer people, then one of us has to go."

The words came down like a sledgehammer - a sledgehammer of truth that Tim didn't want to admit. The two men were at loggerheads over the direction of the company and were tearing it apart at the seams. The company didn't need Tim and he knew it. The company, on the other hand, did need Peter. He was the face of the changes that the industry has been seeing. He'd made some of the hard decisions already and the market was respecting the company for what they'd done.

"So how's that going to work?" Tim's voice was calmer but his shaking hands were telling a different story.

"Tim, if these people can't operate without you after all these years, then they aren't the right people. I think they feel they can - and quite frankly, if they can't then they should never have been on the team in the first place." Peter's answer made it clear who had to go.

Tim was quiet. He sat in silence. Peter looked at Tim's face and for the first time, saw the wear and tear of age. He had known Tim for many years but had only been his partner for a couple. The old Tim he knew seemed to have disappeared, replaced by someone who feared the end, feared making a mistake that could cost him everything, and feared losing what was left of what he had built. Though the deal the two men struck in the beginning cost Tim hundreds of thousands of dollars, there was still a chance of losing more. Losing everything.

Peter remained quiet as well. He understood that this decision was not what was really needed. This too, like the bandaid solution of more money, would only help for a short period. He had already spoken to the team asking what they needed from Tim and it had been clear that Tim's relevance to the daily operations was small. Also, Peter's gut instinct told him it wouldn't last. The day the deal was signed, Tim had said he wanted to move on, but as the months came and went, the legal reins were never handed over. As much as Peter as President, could fire him, Tim still controlled the legal entity.

Peter found no comfort in what had happened but silently thanked Ling for helping him remember that his personal space was in his control. Maybe this time, the message would be heard and the reins would be handed over.

Chapter Nine – Clearing the Images

Absolutely exhausted from a long week fraught with challenges on all fronts, including the removal of Tim, Peter started the 83 mile drive again. Last week's lesson had opened his eyes to many things. Practising the personal space thing was difficult but Peter felt he got results. Understanding what he could and couldn't control shed light on many areas. He even began to realize he was trying to control others at work and at home. The office picked up on Peter's new found understanding and some commented on his calmness and concentration.

"I think it's working," Peter said out loud to an empty car. "I don't know what I'm doing but something is happening."

The drive was easy and he made it in record time. Since he was well ahead of schedule he decided to just park outside Ling's office and watch.

Within minutes, Peter was feeling surprised by the neighbourhood and wondered why he hadn't noticed everything before. The streets were busy. People were walking and laughing and talking. It was an actual community of mostly Asian shops and people. Peter saw that there was a true neighbourliness happening.

His awareness continued as he saw that there appeared to be an unspoken trust of the people. Shopkeepers wares were arranged on the sidewalks. Fruits, vegetables, knickknacks, almost everything you could want. Each shop having handmade signs and unpriced items, obviously there waiting for the bargaining to begin.

He rolled down his window to capture the sounds. The language was fast and for him, completely incomprehensible, but there was no need for words. The energy was obvious; the movement of the street appeared chaotic but was in perfect harmony. Peter was captivated by the organized chaos.

Snapping out of the trance, he realized it was time to see Ling. Stepping out of the car he considered not locking it. “Okay, now,” Peter said. “Don’t get carried away. This is still reality and in reality people do bad things.”

Peter walked the stairs and took time to ‘notice.’ Fully determined to be on his game, he was warming up his brain, thinking as he walked: ‘Fifteen steps per floor, except the 4rd floor, which has 16. What’s up with that? Red carpet with green paisley pattern. How could I have missed that before? Seven steps were missing the gold twist rod that held back the carpet. At least I think seven. Next time I will be sure.’ At each level a wooden door blocked the corridor of offices. Exit signs above the entries amused him as they were on the wrong side of the door. “Exit to where?” he said aloud.

Six flights of stairs. Proud as a peacock, Peter reviewed how many things he’d noticed in just six flights of stairs. Seemingly useless information but this time he could show Ling that he was noticing life. He let out a loud “Ha” that echoed down the stairwell.

UNIT 625 Ling HO – MEDITATION MASTER

Peter threw open the door in his confident way and was instantly taken aback. There were three other people in the room.

His face flushed red and his breathing stopped.

“Oh sorry,” he said.

A wave of emotion rushed through him. He felt embarrassed like he’d been caught seeing a ‘therapist’. Anxiety hit him like a brick wall, but then optimism kicked in. ‘These people must be leaving’, he thought. Realizing that his hand was still on the door knob and the fight or flight instinct was all he could think of, he gave his head a shake, stepped in and closed the door behind him. Peter gave three polite nods, accompanied by two "Hey's" and one "How ya doing?". His intros were complete.

The three, who obviously knew each other, smiled and properly introduced themselves.

Teri, mid-fifties, beautiful and slim with a soft handshake and amazing eyes. Having spent her entire life with people judging her outer beauty, she struggled to make people understand and respect her inner qualities. At the same time, she knew her past was littered with times when she'd used that outer being to ease her path in life and she now felt the roughness in the road that came from playing down her physical presence. Little did she know her beauty was alive throughout. Many recognized that fact, but few had told her.

Alice, early forties, shy but extremely caring and gentle. Her training in meditation had awoken her and she now found herself in a one-way marriage. Spending 15 years caring for and doting on her husband, she was longing for the same in return but feared asking that of him. Her spirit was pure and her ability to experience life now was keenly awake.

Sandra, late forties but looking late fifties, confident, classy and definitely a 'driver' judging by the way she approached Peter. She had seen a lot and weathered every storm she'd faced. She'd taken up meditation to help her slow down as she was addicted to the drama of life. Finding peace in not-knowing was her desire, but her DNA demanded that she always be right and let no man, woman or beast, know more than she did. Her internal struggle was definitely active.

"What's your name?" Teri finally asked.

"Oh, sorry. Peter." he replied, instantly realizing he'd used another 'sorry' and hoping Ling hadn't heard.

"Don't be sorry," Sandra said and all three laughed. Obviously they all knew Ling.

Taking a deep breath, Peter got control of himself and asked, "Are you three here to meet Ling?"

"Yes," they responded in unison.

"Oh, I must have mixed up my meeting time."

From the back room Ling's voice pierced the conversation, "No, you have the correct time Peter."

Ling appeared walking slowly to the front of the room. Hugs were exchanged between Ling and the three ladies and Peter got a polite bow. Ling continued, "Peter, this is Teri, Alice and Sandra. They are also students of mine, taking Level Seven meditation. They asked for a refresher on today's lesson so I invited them to join us. Are you okay with that?"

Scared stiff Peter said, "Absolutely" then thought to himself: 'Level Seven, holy crap! I'm like Level Zero.' And with that his confidence from the stairs evaporated.

"Great" Ling said. "Don't worry. They don't bite."

"I might" said Sandra with a wicked smile and a bone rattling laugh.

Alice quickly chimed in, "Behave Sandra".

'Oh what have I done? I am crazy!' Peter's internal conversation was in full swing again.

They walked together to a larger room on the right. This one was tastefully decorated, in what Peter thought would be a meditation guru's taste. There was the same carpeted floors and church basement chairs, but this time there were nice big pillows in the corners, a table in the middle with a burning candle and a Tibetan bowl. Peter saw the bowl and was proud of himself for knowing what it was but had no idea what to do with it. The air was soothing with an elusive scent.

"Sage," Alice said, apparently noticing Peter's nose in the air.

"Thanks," he said with a smile.

There were five chairs this time. Peter picked one of the chairs in the middle, not wanting to be first or last on the ends.

The ladies were still chatting as if Peter wasn't there; smiling, laughing, and offering soothing comments, depending on the story of the moment. Very clearly this was a summary of their week's events.

Ling came in, sat in the teacher's chair, smiled and said a pleasant "Good Afternoon".

"Good afternoon," they replied in near harmony.

Ling looked directly at Teri and asked, "So Teri, how are you?"

"Great thank you," she replied.

Ling kept his focus on her to see if she would add narrative but when it was clear she wouldn't, he moved on.

Skipping Peter, he looked at Alice.

"Alice," said Ling.

"Ling," she replied.

"Having a good week?" he asked.

"It's okay," was her answer. Short and sweet.

"Okay" Ling replied and then looked to Sandra.

All Peter could think of was: 'What?! Where is his 'don't judge it' crap or his deep 'are you sure?' probing questions?'

"And Sandra, how are you?"

"Exceptional, Ling. How are you?"

"Very well, thank you."

Now Ling's eyes were on Peter who took a minute to realize this and snapped to attention.

"Welcome, Peter." Ling said with purity and softness.

"Thanks, Ling," he replied.

"How was your week?"

"It was okay too," he replied with a quick acknowledgement of Alice beside him.

Ling smirked, obviously wanting to probe deeper, and said, "Okay, then let's begin."

"Close your eyes, find your center, that ball of light in the center of your heart."

Peter's was dumbfounded, thinking, 'What? Already? No lead-in, no today we-are-going-to? Hey man, I'm not Level Seven. I've just been doing this for a few weeks. Hello!'

Peter tried to catch up as Ling rapidly continued. "Today we are going to learn how to clear the images in our mind and how to create mock-ups," Ling began the narrative Peter was seeking. "It is very important that you 'experience' a clear mind and then learn the role of mock-ups. I want you to create a container in front of you. Visualize the container. See its colour, its texture, the shape, the material, edges, everything. Admire its beauty. Admire your creation. Take pride in the beauty you have created."

Peter's thoughts were lost, 'What kind of container? Shipping container? Box? Lunch kit? I think this is what he means.' Peter thought as he created a vase. 'Really? A vase? All the containers in the world and I create a vase?' His brain once again was in full gear.

Ling cut the silence. "Don't judge it, just notice its beauty. Whatever you have created is perfect. If it's a box, it's perfect. An envelope, it's perfect; a cup, it's perfect; a basket, it's perfect."

Silence again. To Peter it seemed like time was dragging on. 'What am I to do now?' he wondered. 'Okay...maybe I will sneak a peek.' He opened his left eye and saw Teri sitting straight, eyes closed smile on her face, glowing actually. She was truly enjoying the creation in her head. His thoughts wavered back and forth between 'Okay, they're all freaks' to 'Why can't I feel that way?' He closed his eyes again and started to refocus on the vase he'd created, trying to find some joy when...

Ling said, "Now destroy it! Crumple it up, torch it, blow it up. Destroy your creation. Notice how you feel. Don't judge your feelings, just notice them."

Ling said with authority, "Now create another container. Notice it. Is it big? Half open? Fully open? Closed tight? Admire its beauty, its colour, its texture."

A couple of minutes went by and Ling added the expected, "Now destroy it. Throw it away. Cut it up. Whatever you want to do." Pausing for everyone to enjoy their destruction, he said. "And let's create a third container. Notice it. This time we will do something different. I want you to think of the first person that comes to your mind. Whoever it is."

Tim instantly sprang into Peter's mind.

Ling continued, "Now put their image in the container. And destroy the container."

With that Peter smiled, but soon caught himself smiling and immediately stopped.

Ling noticed Peter's smile and said, "Find the humor and peace in the destruction. You are taking with that image all of the crap that is left behind. With this you are simply disconnecting the energy with this individual. In this disconnection you can both have more clarity and peace." Giving everyone a minute to absorb what he is saying he pushed forward, "You are not hurting them, only setting them free. You are removing the lingering memory or energy of your last encounters."

With this Peter seemed to remove the guilt of destroying his partner.

Ling, sensing that everyone had destroyed their containers, said: "Now create another one. Put all your worries of tomorrow and your thoughts of yesterday into the container."

Peter's mind instantly built a list to go for a ride in his new envelope, which was the container of choice for this round of destruction.

Ling cut in, "And destroy it." He pauses for several minutes allowing everyone to do the work. Then calmly states, "Open your eyes and come out of meditation."

Once Ling saw everyone looking at him, he began his questions, "So Teri, how was that?"

"Good," she answered. "It's been a while since I took the time to really clear the mind."

"And how did it feel?" Ling asked.

"Great! I was really enjoying the creation and really looking at it, fully knowing I was going to destroy it."

Ling smiled.

"Alice," he asked. "How about you?"

"I struggled with it," she said meekly. "It was always the same image coming back. I'd think I was rid of it and there it would be again!"

Ling laughed, "Kind of like life, heh?"

With that, even Peter smiled. Many times he'd ended a conversation or situation only to find it returning unaltered.

"And Sandra..." Ling asked.

"Loved it" she said. "Rapid fire, people going in, and me destroying. Easy."

"Good." Ling said, but his eyes looked doubtful.

"So Peter?" Ling looked solely at him. "How was it for you?"

"It was alright," Peter replied. "I liked the destroying part, especially when the people were there." Noticing what he'd said he quickly began to apologize as the ladies smiled and laughed with empathy.

"I mean, it seemed to allow me to forget about the memory that was lingering regarding that person," Peter continued trying to sound like a sane human being, but feeling he was failing. He tried to answer again: "It seemed to free up brain space with each container."

"Exactly," all four affirmed with enthusiasm.

Ling's voice quickly cut through the excitement. "That is the point of this meditation Peter. You need that 'brain space' as you call it to allow you to 'be' in this moment. Thinking of what happened in the past ties up your creativity and your potential. Best of all, it allows you to do what we will learn next, which is mock-ups. But be careful not to use this for anything other than clearing the mind. This is not for destruction or for anger. It is an exercise in creating beauty, putting memories in that beauty and then clearing the mind. It does not mean you are hurting them, nor that you will forget them forever. It is to clear your mind so you can BE. It is to acknowledge the image and then let it go." Ling paused to ensure his message had been received and then continued: "Let's go back into meditation. Close your eyes, center, ground. Just check to ensure your energy is flowing. Create a quick container, put the conversations of the past 15 minutes into it and destroy it. Now I want you to create a mock-up. Peter, a mock-up is merely a picture of the future inside a clear helium balloon. It's like how you dream the future to be. The mock-up picture is what you want to see yourself doing in the future. Envision the picture. What do you look like? What are you doing? Be very detailed."

With strength and conviction in his voice, Ling said, “Be very sure it is in your highest integrity. Breathe. See it. When you have it nicely defined and the picture is clear, let your balloon float away. If this is in your highest integrity and the highest integrity of the universe, it will be so.”

Peter was puzzled and didn’t understand.

“Open your eyes, and come out of meditation.” Ling ended his speech.

Again when Ling saw that everyone was ready, he asked “Questions?”

Peter thought: ‘Questions? Are you kidding me? What was that all about?’ He sat in silence trying to hear what each person was saying but all he heard was his own voice inside his head.

Then Ling said, “Thank you very much everyone. I hope you have a great week.”

And with that Peter snapped awake and realized that the lesson was over. Bewildered, he got up with everyone else, said the customary good-byes, blindly walked down the same stairs he had noticed so vividly an hour ago and got into his car.

On the drive home, doubt kicked in heavily for Peter, ‘How could I think I was doing so well when I clearly suck at this? Maybe clarity isn’t what it’s cracked up to be.’

Ling HO – MEDITATION

MASTER TEACHINGS

Lesson One

- See ball of light and move into center of heart.
- Connect cord from butt to earth.
- When I control my space and clear everything out I will then be able to find the answer.

Lesson Two

- Do lesson one over again.
- Focus on what is behind what you see.
- Block other things out and notice.
- Watch how people act and hear the words that come to mind.
- Be attuned to where on your body you feel something when the descriptors come up.
- Do <u>NOT</u> judge (very hard).
- Be aware that many things are happening at the same time as you are happening.

BE IN THE MOMENT

Lesson Three – CHAKRAS

Big lesson today! Gut feeling, headaches, control

- Your personal space is the only circle of control.
- The personal space (aka aura) surrounds body like an energy field approximately an arm's length around body.
- Energy flows up from ground, down from universe.
- My personal energy flows around me and through my "CHAKRAS".

- 7 Chakras
    - 1st – privates - survival
    - 2nd – belly button - emotions & sensuality/sexuality
    - 3rd - solar plexus – gut feeling, purpose, control
    - 4th – heart – love others & self
    - 5th – throat – communication
    - 6th – forehead – clairvoyance
    - 7th – top of head – knowingness, enlightenment
- When I feel something like a lump in my throat I first acknowledge the feeling, try to understand it and then move it through my body and down my grounding. *ASK Ling MORE*
- Thinking can lead to justifying. True answer is usually in first feeling.

Lesson Four

- Put thoughts in a container and destroy the container?
- Put dreams in a balloon and let them go?
- Realize you are crazy!

Chapter Ten - Quitting

Still confused and doubtful from the last 'session' with Ling, Peter worked hard to find an excuse not to meet Ling the next week. It turned out that Peter didn't have to work very hard at all. The office didn't even react to Tim's departure as they were all gearing up for the following week when everyone would be in town for national meetings.

Since the group thing with the ladies, Peter hadn't even thought of meditation, clarity, balloons, containers or anything. His sole focus was on preparing for everyone next week.

All team members were working hard to get their projects done as they were soon to embark on days of long, tedious meetings - meetings that would probably not have positive outcomes. Since last quarter, layoffs had again been necessary and the economy was still tight. Competitors were getting hungry and prices were starting to drop.

Peter wasn't looking forward to next week either. Everyone seemed depressed, grudgingly getting their work done, ensuring they were not going to be the next to go, but not showing any passion. People were sticking to the rules so they could say "Done" when asked for a progress report at Monday's meeting.

Kirsten entered Peter's office, walking and talking: "All the numbers are in except Kevin's." Kevin was a 26 year-old sales rep who was truly struggling. Kirsten oversaw all reporting and just couldn't understand why Kevin continued to miss targets and then deadlines for reporting.

"How can that be, Kirsten?" Peter said aggressively. She instinctively looked down and became quiet. Immediately Ling's voice rang out in Peter's head: 'Look Peter, look. Don't just see, look!' "Kirsten, sorry, this has nothing to do with you. Thank you." Peter said calmly. He stopped and thought: 'What is the real issue with Kevin? And how the heck did Ling's voice get inside my head?'

Peter put the numbers on the side of his desk and got back to his preparations. His workload had now increased. Even though most of the daily operations hadn't involved Tim, some of the tasks he did now fell on Peter's desk.

Matt was next to come to Peter. Matt was the operations manager and these meetings were mostly about his agenda. He walked in without knocking or even a greeting. "There's no way we can get this whole agenda into four days," he said.

Peter didn't stop working, but replied, "Then we need to prepare the team for longer days. We have to get everything done. There's no option."

"Longer days! No way!" Matt shouted.

"Pardon me?" Peter said with a don't-forget-who-you-are-talking-to look. Matt picked up on the look, turned around and left the office. Peter wasn't really sure if Matt was going back to his desk or out the front door. There was no time to do anything about it in any case, so Peter got back to work.

"Bing" the computer's you've-got-mail sound broke his stride. Strange. He was sure he turned it off, as he often did when he needed to get his work done. Looking at the monitor, he wasn't surprised to see an email from Ling.

SUBJECT LINE: *This week's lesson.*

Body of the email: *Remember to breathe Peter, just breathe. See you next week. Ling.*

"Freaky little guy," Peter said out loud. "Okay, I'll try this meditation thing and prove it won't work for me. We will never meet again, Ling."

Peter got up, walked to his office door and quietly closed and locked it. 'Don't want anyone seeing this.' he thought and smiled. He sat on the leather couch and closed his eyes attempting to focus. Now that a few weeks had gone by, he knew the routine. He put the ball of light in the middle of his heart and tried hard to see this 'grounding thing.'

The process actually seemed to slow Peter down a bit. He realized his breathing was easier and his shoulders were looser. He smiled as he found himself doing the Rafiki finger/thumb touch thing! He struggled to wash his personal space but went through the motions anyway. Then the pictures started coming. His mind was showing him pictures of all the people who had interrupted his day. 'Wow, how do I get anything done?' he wondered.

He created one of those containers and put all of the interruptions in it. After acknowledging them, he torched the container. 'Char-broiled. Ashes. Ya!', the smile on his face widened.

Clearly feeling better, he opted for a few more minutes of breathing and then slowly opened his eyes. He sat on the couch and looked around, not thinking of anything, just being at peace. Fully content, he walked to the door and calmly opened it to the chaos that was his company.

First stop...Matt.

"Hey Matt," Peter said after taking a seat in one of the chairs.

"Hey," he replied without looking up. Slouched over his keyboard, Matt looked barely alive.

"Let's see that agenda." Peter calmly said. "Maybe we can lighten a few items or break out some sessions."

Matt's shoulders came up and there seemed to be an increase of light in the room.

'Look Peter. Look.' Ling's voice rang again in Peter's head.

Matt's demeanour changed instantly, as if Peter had just thrown him a life preserver.

"I think these items here can be cut 25 percent and these can run concurrently," Matt explained as he slid the four-page document across the desk.

Peter's aggression kicked in and he instantly thought: 'Why didn't you say that when you came in rather than losing your cool?!' But then, 'Breathe Peter, breathe', came in loud and clear.

The voice in his head caused a smile, he looked at Matt's recommendations and replied, "I trust you, Matt. You know this better than I do. Rerun the agenda with those recommendations and bring it by after lunch. I'll quickly review and you can send it out."

Matt beamed with relief.

"Sound good, Matt?" Peter asked.

"Sounds great Peter. I'll do it now."

Next stop...Kirsten.

Kirsten held this whole place together. She was the conduit of every project and every report. Peter knew that he needed her on-side or he would have trouble on his hands.

“Kirsten, you got a second?” he asked at her doorway.

Typing away at lightning speed, she answered without skipping a beat. “In two minutes I will. Just need to get this last email out the...door...and...yes... I am ready.” Talking and typing with ease and grace, saying 12 words but typing 100.

“How are you doing?” Peter asked the standard question, but this time noticing how her body and especially her eyes reacted to the question.

“Good,” she replied looking directly at him.

This time he picked up on the ‘Good’ as being more like ‘I’m good as long as I get a chance to kill about eight people in this office and then go home and sleep for a month.’ Peter smiled, ‘Thanks Ling’.

“Okay,” he gently laughed, “Let’s get some stuff off your plate. What do you need to complete today?” With that question he tried Ling’s suggestion to ‘Notice the feeling you get in your body. Where is it?’

The front of Peter’s forehead started to tingle as she flipped through papers on her desk and then said “No, Peter. Seriously. I’m good. It will all get done.”

With that answer his head started to pound and he thought, ‘Time for me to help her see what she can’t see. Clearly she is up against the tree.’ He paused but then said in a strong and understanding way, “I know it will Kirsten. You are the master of multitasking and I see you are in eighth gear. But let’s use Shelly to help you with the stuff that doesn’t need your mastery or training.”

Shelly was a bright girl too. She hadn't been with the company long but she had the ability to take any task and get it done. Peter could feel his throat tighten slightly as he saw Kirsten's jaw clench and her eyes squint. He held back from saying anything more and let her process her thoughts.

'It's like a mirror,' Ling's words came again. 'What is she showing you and why does your throat now hurt?'

"Say it, Kirsten," Peter said. "Whatever it is, say it." Peter could see her energy build up like a bull ready to send a stupid cowboy over the rodeo rails.

"These guys are going to kill me, Peter. How many times do I need to show them how to do this stuff? Use Shelly? Sure, but she'll just be frustrated too! Do you want her to take this crap on? Seriously? Sounds great! Take it! I have the seven reports for you, eight major projects due, and we can't seem to get any clients to sign off on things..." She rattled off a huge list.

'Clear the mind. Acknowledge and release.' Ling was back again.

As she threw each item out, Peter created containers in his head, putting the things on her to-do list into the containers and blowing them up. Kirsten's list starts to dwindle and Peter's container creation followed suit. He couldn't believe how strong he felt. Kirsten had just thrown a barrage of to-do's at him that would normally have caused him to say: "Well you should see what I have to do!" but instead he'd destroyed each item. Not only did he feel better, but Kirsten was smiling from ear to ear.

"Wow that felt good," she said.

"Yes it did" he laughed back.

"Okay. If you can spare Shelly, I can use her help." Kirsten said.

"Done," he replied. "She's all yours for the day."

"Thanks Peter," Kirsten said as Peter left her office.

"No worries," he replied while taking two seconds to notice that his throat and forehead were fine. Walking past Shelly's desk he said, "Shelly, Kirsten could use a hand. Take anything she can give you and do your best as always."

"Sure," she replied happily.

"Make sure she gives you something that challenges you," he continued. And with that he could see Shelly's pride jump a notch.

Next stop...Kevin

'Breathe, center, ground,' Ling's voice reappeared as Peter walked down the hall past the rows of cubicles. Kevin was pounding away at his keyboard with his phone glued to his ear. Peter sat in an empty cubicle – the remains of the last cut backs. He sat quietly and though he pretended to be focused on his iPhone, he tuned his ears to Kevin's words and tried to notice what came up.

Peter determined that Kevin was talking to a new prospect and trying to get a meeting. His voice was rapid and he was saying the words he'd been taught, but something was missing. Kevin had such potential - he reminded Peter of some of the best reps he'd known when he was young. His mind wandered backward 20 years to the path he'd been on. His entire body lit up - especially down low in what Ling called the first chakra. Peter suddenly snapped back to the moment at hand and he struggled to remember what the first chakra means.

"Survival" he said out loud. Kevin looked at him as did others in the sales area.

Peter waved his hand and everyone went back to work. Kevin, clearly rattled now, sped up the pace of his conversation, obviously thinking Peter was speaking to him. The pressure of lower sales had been an issue for months and with him at the bottom, Peter could understand why he got rattled.

Peter wrote a note and placed in front of Kevin, 'Slow it down, build the value of you, close for a meeting. No rush.' Then he left the room so Kevin could focus on what needed to be done.

Heading back to his desk the word 'Survival' kept reappearing. He closed his door, sat down and pulled out the notes from Ling's sessions. Personal space, first chakra, circle of control, survival, grounded, ball of light. All these words jumped off the page like they were being highlighted just for him. He started to connect all of Ling's teachings with many things he had been taught in the past. The feeling in his first chakra was a constant pain. He tried to envision Ling in the room and with that he centered, grounded, and focused on his own energy.

Peter envisioned the word "Survival" up in front of him and he could feel his body slouch. 'What comes up for you is what you are feeling.' Ling's voice was ringing in his ear.

Sludge. Black, brown, mucky sludge, gross sticky crap. That's what was coming up. 'Push through it.' Ling's voice echoed again. Peter focused fully on the sludge. He tried to make it speed up so he could flow it down his grounding. 'Focus Peter,' Ling's words were still there, 'Look, don't just see.' Peter waited as a ton of images come to mind. Kevin, Matt, Shelly, Kirsten and the rest of the team, including Tim. Even Maslow's hierarchy pyramid was vivid in front of him. He created a giant container and dumped everything in it. More than once. Then, when confident that everything and everyone was in there, he crumpled it up.

Then he turned his focus to the sludge. Like a Star Wars episode, he imagined energy breaking up the sludge until it was gone and it was replaced with water. He basked in the flow of the water, sitting still with it for a few minutes before he opened his eyes and looked around. Forty-five minutes had gone by and he felt amazing. Better yet, Peter now thought he was getting it. 'We are all worried about survival and with that we can't see anything good. Do I dare try one of those balloons? What did Ling call them? Mock-ups I think. Yeah, mock-ups. Okay, here goes. Center, ground, balance, clear that space! Create the balloon, and let's draw the picture.' He saw himself leading through empowerment, leading the way he'd been taught, from the books and from the streets. He saw the company prospering and targets being achieved.

'I like it,' he thought. 'Now what did Ling say to do? Oh yeah, be sure it is in the highest integrity of the universe and then let it go! Float away balloon, float away!'

Peter opened his eyes and came out of meditation. He gave a silent nod of pride while he moved to his desk. "Now let's get through this," he said as he grabbed the top piece of paper from the pile.

As the day came to an end, he pulled the team together and calmly spoke to them. Reading each person's body language and 'energy', he tried to speak to all, yet penetrate each.

"Hey team," he started, "thanks for a huge effort today and for the past six months. It has been a tough run but we are here. You made it. You did. I can tell that each of you had a separate and equally tough journey to get here. The next few days will be ones that will frustrate you but hopefully will also inspire you. Get some rest this weekend. Clear your mind of all your troubles and let's start fresh on Monday. No one comes in this weekend, okay?" He waited for each person to look him in the eye and say yes.

When everyone left the room, he took out his pad and though he hadn't had an official lesson, he wrote what he'd learned.

MASTER TEACHINGS

Lesson One

- See ball of light and move into center of heart.
- Connect cord from butt to earth.

Lesson Two

- Do lesson one over again.
- Focus on what is behind what you see.
- Block other things out and notice.
- Watch how people act and hear the words that come to mind.
- Be attuned to where on your body you feel something when the descriptors come up.
- Do <u>NOT</u> judge (very hard).
- Be aware that many things are happening at the same time as you are happening.

BE IN THE MOMENT

Lesson Three – CHAKRAS

Big lesson today! Gut feeling, headaches, control.

- Your personal space is the only circle of control.
- The personal space (aka aura) surrounds body like an energy field approximately an arm's length around body.
- Energy flows up from ground, down from universe.
- My personal energy flows around me and through my "CHAKRAS".
- 7 Chakras
    - 1st – privates - survival
    - 2nd – belly button - emotions & sensuality/sexuality
    - 3rd - solar plexus – gut feeling, purpose, control
    - 4th – heart – love others & self
    - 5th – throat – communication
    - 6th – forehead – clairvoyance
    - 7th – top of head – knowingness, enlightenment
- When I feel something like a lump in my throat I first acknowledge the feeling, try to understand it and then move it through my body and down my grounding. *ASK Ling MORE*
- Thinking can lead to justifying. True answer is usually in first feeling.

- When I control my space and clear everything out I will then be able to find the answer.

Lesson Four

- Put thoughts in a container and destroy the container?
- Put dreams in a balloon and let them go?
- Realize you are crazy!

Lesson Five

- Take the time to look at the people you work with. Give them time to process their emotions.
- Understand their situation, see how that reflects your own situation.
- LEAD through empowerment. Have them use their energy towards the goal.
- Create a vision of what you want and if it's in the "highest integrity" let it go.

Chapter Eleven – Integrity & Intention

Saturday morning and Peter was awake at 4 am. Normally an early riser, but even for him, this was early. The house was silent. He sat quietly in bed and tried to do the meditation thing again.

Closing his eyes, he imagined a ball of light. It was a bright light directly in front of him. He moved it swiftly between his eyes to the center of his head. He envisioned his grounding cord, remembering it as a cable connected from the base of his spine to the center of the earth. He hooked in the cable and grounded himself. Ensuring it was flowing, he looked at the flow and tried hard not to judge it, just making sure it was flowing down the grounding cord. 'Time for the cleaning. Wow, there's a bit of crap in there now.' he thought as he did the work.

He sat in pure silence acknowledging all that came to mind. Whatever it was, he didn't judge it, just acknowledged it. Slowly this time, he made sure all his thoughts were gone.

Nothing else was on his mind. Pure silence. He sat for what felt like an hour but was actually only ten minutes, then a clear question appeared. "Am I acting in the highest integrity of the universe?"

No answer came, but a parade of images did - memories that built arguments for both sides of the debate. He stopped the parade with 'What does Ling actually mean by highest integrity of the universe?' And with that question, Peter opened his eyes, came out of meditation and got out of bed.

Making his way through the stillness and the darkness he found his iPhone. One quick email to Ling:

'Hello Ling. Thanks for the email yesterday, it actually helped. Not that I am surprised. I was wondering if you could spare a few minutes this weekend? Next week I have everyone in town for meetings so I was hoping we could connect before Monday. Sorry, I have a question for you! I bet that surprises you. LOL.'

He headed to the kitchen to make an espresso when his phone said 'Bing! Don't ignore me - you have a message.'

It was Ling.

'Glad to hear it helped. Of course I have time to talk, even meet in person if you prefer. Let me know what time works for you. And Peter... we all have questions, so never be sorry. It is the answers that we seek which determine how our journey unfolds.'

With that Peter had a dilemma. He wanted to meet with Ling but it was Saturday and that meant today was family day.

"Was that Ling?" Marie asked from the stairs.

"Yep," Peter replied.

"Go," she said.

"Go where?" he asked, knowing what she meant.

"Meet Ling. Go meet with Ling. You are no use to us here if you're thinking of being there. We'll be fine. Come back ready to be with us, that's all I ask."

Marie was always right. She'd been by Peter's side for over twenty years and could read his energy better than Ling could.

"Okay. I will be back before Sam's practice." He replied. "And Marie...thanks."

"Yah, yah," she said with a smile and headed back to bed.

Peter quickly responded to Ling's email with *"How about in an hour or so? I can head out now and with no traffic, I can be there in just over an hour."*

Ling replied, *"Now works, but not at my office. Sun will be up in about 45 minutes. Let's go to Pier 19. It's about half-way between us. Do you know the place?"*

"Yes, that's perfect." And Peter headed out the front door to make his way there.

Pier 19 is the only pier in the inlet where you can face east. Peter couldn't help but think that the dark drive was a calm reminder of what happens when you deal with your issues. The darkness was there but it was never perfectly black. Sooner or later the sun would come up.

Peter was closer to Pier 19 than Ling was, so he took a bit longer to do the drive - actually taking the time to notice and look. He parked the car and walked to the Pier. Fully expecting to be there first, he was surprised to see Ling standing at the end overlooking the water. "Surprised" is a strong word...actually, it was more like "I-should-have-known."

"Good morning, Ling." Peter quietly greeted his master.

"It will be in about five minutes," said Ling, nodding towards the glow coming over the trees in the horizon.

"True enough," Peter replied. "Thanks for coming out here to meet me. I thought I would arrive before you, so I dawdled a bit. Sorry... um thanks." Peter hated the word 'sorry' by this point.

"Peter, you are welcome but no thanks are needed. I was already here," said Ling, holding up his iPhone. "I come here nearly every morning. Been coming since Sue Li died seven years ago." He continued, "We all have our things that keep us up at night Peter. Sue Li is mine."

With that, Peter saw Ling Ho as a human after all - a man no different than him. A bit freaky, but just a man getting through this life with the rest of us. "Then, thanks for sharing this time and place with me Ling." Peter replied, "I appreciate it."

"You are very welcome. Isn't that easier than saying sorry?" He smiled. "We all say 'sorry', thinking we are inconveniencing others. Sometimes it's warranted, so do not get me wrong, but when you are saying sorry, you really mean "thank you" and that's hard to say. Accepting, welcoming, and appreciating help is what the ego fights every moment. Destruction of the ego allows a person to be thankful for every breath they take. In that thankfulness, being sorry is never warranted. Not only does the ego not have food to feed off, but guilt has no place to fester. Ego and guilt, Peter, those are lifelong lessons even I have not mastered." He took a breath, "But you had a question and it must have been important to drive 30 minutes to ask it, so... ask away!"

Peter stood speechless as he had never heard Ling speak uninterrupted before. 'Holy smokes,' he thought. 'That was a ton of information in one breath.' There had been no questions in Ling's speech. Peter listened attentively to ensure he captured everything, then when he knew Ling was finished, he spoke: "My question is simple, but I think the answer will be complex so I 'appreciate' you meeting me today to chat. When doing mock-ups, what do you mean by 'in the highest integrity of the universe'?"

Ling looked out over the sunrise and merely nodded his head in the direction of the trees. The sun's white hue had broken the surface.

The trees were glowing yellow. The water was alive and the sky was an amazing blue. The light fog along the shores was moving as the breath of the Earth. Peter had never 'seen' anything like it. It was as if the Earth had awoken from her rest and was beginning again. A fresh start. Ling's eyes were closed, his face to the sun, chin in the air, pure calm. He began: "Peter, there is an integrity in everything we do, think, or say. We are given a great gift and that gift is life, a chance to be here on the Earth with other people, animals, plants, beings. How we act, interact, and react has an impact on everything. Everything. The ego's job is to ensure you feed it. It is the ego that gives you 'flashes of excitement'. It is integrity that gives you a 'lifetime of excitement'. It is the ego that gets you 'things', it is integrity that gets you 'abundance'. It is the ego that gets you popularity but it is integrity that gets you friends. It is the ego that gives you pain and pleasure, and it is integrity that allows you to experience pain and pleasure. Doing something with the highest integrity of the universe is doing something that is as ego-free as humanly possible. You see Peter, the ego is a part of a person like an arm, leg or foot. We all have one and, like a body part, we can control it. When the ego controls us we lose integrity and even though the benefits of the ego are so great and they are very appealing, without the integrity they are merely flashes in the pan! Look back on your life Peter. Do a stock-check on your wins and losses as you call them. Judge them and ask, was it ego-based or integrity-based? Doing things the way of integrity is not easy and is sometimes not very fruitful in the moment but I can guarantee it feels a lot better."

Ling smiled. "Whether you call it coincidence, luck, timing, whatever, the universe will ensure that you get the message. Until you come to terms with acting in the highest integrity of the universe, you will find that your journey is like a ride on a severe rollercoaster. Your ups will be counterbalanced by your downs and when I get to the "Karma" lesson, you will realize the downs are very deep and the ups are very steep and they come at a cost. They cost you and your family. Your family is part of your universe – is what you do in the highest integrity of your family?"

Pausing to let this all sink in, Ling took a deep breath and continued, "So when we do mock-ups, they are somewhat like goal setting and dreams with one big difference. A mock-up can have the entire universe on your side to manifest that dream. Can you imagine the entire universe on your team?"

Peter nodded but didn't speak. He knew Ling was not finished.

Ling had not broken his view of the sunrise during this entire soliloquy. He continued, "Acting in the highest integrity of the universe allows you to experience the moment you are in. To realize that the moment you just left behind was one you needed to have in order to be in this moment. Acting in the highest integrity of the universe helps you realize that every person around you is here for a reason and you can either find out why or just ignore it. That is up to you. Acting in the highest integrity of the universe gives clarity, Peter. Clarity. The fog is gone. The Earth is awake. The sun is spotlighting things for you. It is up to you to see them."

And with that, there was silence. They both looked out on the water, the shore, and the trees and they just breathed. Ling started again, this time, looking directly at Peter as if into his very soul, "Your intentions, Peter, must be in the highest integrity of the universe. For you to have the clarity you seek, you must clean your mind and set intentions that the universe wants to support. Your family integrity, your employee integrity, your customer integrity, your fiscal integrity, your personal integrity, the planet's integrity and the universal integrity all must be considered to the utmost of your ability. Those intentions, goals if you will, will manifest. Interactions of the ego will manifest too, but you will pay dearly for following those. Does that answer your question, Peter?"

Rubbing his forehead, Peter slowly replied, "Yes. Yes, it does Ling. Thank you."

"Actually, thank you Peter, because I needed to hear all that for myself too." Ling humbly stated, "Sometimes we all forget why we do the things we do. We all stray from the path and that is part of the journey."

They sat in silence for about another half hour just looking, and, Peter soon realized, meditating. The air was calm and the birds began to sign. A fisherman sat on the rocks and had a different hope for the day, while Peter soaked up everything around him. He understood why Ling came here.

The drive home was easy and calm for Peter. His mind was busy but focused - not focused on what Ling had said, but focused on where he was. He could finally say he was truly 'in the moment'.

He stayed this way for the entire day, watching his kids' activities, listening to Marie's review of her week, even hearing what other kids' parents were actually saying. During a break in the conversation, he smiled as he appreciated that there were actually a few really interesting people in this circle.

Wrapping up the day, he sat with his wine, pen, and pad and summarized the morning lesson.

Ling HO – MEDITATION

MASTER TEACHINGS

Lesson One

- See ball of light and move into center of heart.
- Connect cord from butt to earth.

Lesson Two

- Do lesson one over again.
- Focus on what is behind what you see.
- Block other things out and notice.
- Watch how people act and hear the words that come to mind.
- Be attuned to where on your body you feel something when the descriptors come up.
- Do <u>NOT</u> judge (very hard).
- Be aware that many things are happening at the same time as you are happening.

BE IN THE MOMENT

Lesson Three – CHAKRAS

Big lesson today! Gut feeling, headaches, control.

- Your personal space is the only circle of control.
- The personal space (aka aura) surrounds body like an energy field approximately an arm's length around body.

- Energy flows up from ground, down from universe.
- My personal energy flows around me and through my "CHAKRAS".
- 7 Chakras
    - 1st – privates - survival
    - 2nd – belly button - emotions & sensuality/sexuality
    - 3rd - solar plexus – gut feeling, purpose, control
    - 4th – heart – love others & self
    - 5th – throat – communication
    - 6th – forehead – clairvoyance
    - 7th – top of head – knowingness, enlightenment
- When I feel something like a lump in my throat I first acknowledge the feeling, try to understand it and then move it through my body and down my grounding. *ASK Ling MORE*
- Thinking can lead to justifying. True answer is usually in first feeling.
- When I control my space and clear everything out I will then be able to find the answer.

Lesson Four

- Put thoughts in a container and destroy the container?
- Put dreams in a balloon and let them go?
- Realize you are crazy!

Lesson Five

- Take the time to look at the people you work with. Give them time to process their emotions.
- Understand their situation, see how that reflects in your own situation.
- LEAD through empowerment. Have them use their energy towards the goal.
- Create a vision of what you want and if it's in the "highest integrity" let it go.

Lesson Six

- Highest integrity of the universe is just that, acting in the highest personal integrity of everything around you.
- Ignoring the ego as much as possible.
- Ego-based actions will give faster results, more "things" and quicker pleasures but it will also be short lived and the downside/fall is painful.
- Integrity-based actions will provide lasting results, more abundance and allow me to feel the ups and downs as part of a process to the journey.
- Mock-ups that are in line with integrity will have the aid of the universe. (people, environmental, luck, etc.)

- Mock-ups that are ego-based will not have the universe helping and may even work against you.
- Try a mock-up with integrity while meditating.

Chapter Twelve – Clean Giving and Receiving

Nearly two weeks had gone by and Peter was back in one of Ling's chairs again with the three ladies of 'clearing the mind'. This time when Ling asked how his week was, Peter decided to really let Ling know, "Well, 'no different', I guess, would be the best way to explain it. I did the mock-up that Sunday of how I thought the meetings would go. Acting in the 'highest integrity of the universe' and all that but by the second day, I found myself acting as I have in the past. I got frustrated with a couple of the team members for their lack of not just passion, but even basic 'caring'."

"How did that make you feel?" Ling asked.

"Disappointed. I stayed so calm and positive on the Monday. I gave them extra leeway in all they did so they would feel less stress. I backed off on expectations so they could take the time to think and well, I have to say Ling, the mock-up didn't happen. The universe didn't come together for me."

The three ladies smiled in unison and Alice said, "It happens to us all."

"I'm proud of you Peter," Ling cut in. "It's not easy to meditate and do mock-ups with integrity and then find the results don't manifest. Any idea why they didn't?"

"Well, I assume it is a process that takes time and I have to keep trying." Peter said with a bit of sarcasm in his voice.

"A bit of that Peter, but let's see what else it may be... ladies? Can you relay some insights?"

Alice started, "Mine is with my husband. After the mock-up lesson I went and made him the kindest, gentlest, most loving person I know him to be. My mock-up had him spending time with the family - we were all together laughing, playing and having fun."

"And?" Peter asked.

"Hasn't happened yet." she broke out into full laughter.

Teri stepped in and said, "Peter, we have all experienced exactly what you went through. The significant thing to note is that a mock-up in the highest integrity needs to be pure and clean."

Then it was Sandra's turn to drive it home: "It's about giving and receiving cleanly Peter. Though the goal has integrity at its core, you must be in a place to give and receive cleanly - meaning you must remove judgement of the results."

Confused, Peter looked at Ling, who nodded with his little smile and spoke: "Let's clear it up in meditation. Close your eyes and imagine a ball of light. It is a bright light in the center of your heart. When you have that, imagine your grounding cord. A cord connected from the base of your spine to the center of the earth. Hook in the cable. Ground yourself. Make sure it is flowing. See the flow. Do not judge it - just make sure it is flowing down your grounding cord. Today is about giving and receiving cleanly."

Peter's mind wandered a bit but he brought it back into place. That part was actually getting easier for him.

Ling continued, "This topic is very important as understanding it helps us understand every possible situation that arises. As we all know, our 'circle of control' is our aura and that's all. We have no control over anything else in the universe. We do, however, have the ability to manifest, and manifestation starts with clean giving.

"Giving cleanly is when you 'give' without strings attached. Receiving cleanly is when you 'receive' without strings attached. Think of the last three 'givings' you did, whether it was a candy for your kids, a present for your spouse, or even an extension to a deadline. Was it free and clear (clean as we call it) of conditions or expectations? Did you expect a hug for the candy, a present back from your spouse, or a better report for the extension?"

Hitting home Ling delivered an arrow to Peter's chest.

"And feel how your body reacts when you remember that event. Concentrate on it. Stay grounded. Don't lose yourself to the event, just be the witness, watching it happen."

Peter's eyebrows raised. New territory again. Ling anticipated the confusion his new student would have and so added: "Do not judge it or question it, just witness the event. As you relive the event, notice how your body reacts. Does your energy seem to slow down?"

'Yes it does' Peter said to himself, with a bit of shame for unclean giving, and a bit of pride for being able to feel the energy.

Ling's voice pulled him back. "Increase the flow of your energy, focus on the slowness or the blockage and wash it through."

With that, Peter heard the sound of a tissue being pulled from a box. He could hear and feel Ling walking towards him and thought, 'What's going on?' Then Ling walked away. Keeping his eyes closed, all of Peter's other senses were going strong. He noticed that Alice was fidgeting in the chair beside him. 'Wow, I think this one hit a chord for her.' He returned his focus to himself and the events in his life. The clarity came back fully and he recognised that he did have an expectation to those 'gives'. He sat with that thought and concentrated, 'My first chakra and my third seem tight. No tissue needed here, I'm actually becoming a bit pissed-off. Why can't I have an expectation? I gave them extensions and I let them have the weekend to rest. Can't they at least give back a bit of respect and appreciation and give 110 percent effort!?!'

"Breathe, Peter, breathe." Ling said slowly and calmly, cutting through Peter's thoughts.

Peter let out a huge breath and tried to find that ball of light. It was gone. He worked hard at focusing but it was futile. He began to fidget in his chair, wanting the meditation to end.

Ling stepped in realizing it was time to end the meditation. He calmly states, "When you are ready, open your eyes and come out of meditation."

Peter was first to open his eyes, wanting to move on and get back to real work.

Sandra and Teri acknowledge Ling in unison.

Alice took a bit longer. With red eyes, she opens them and nods to Ling.

Ling's all-knowing face was both comforting and understanding. "So how was that for everyone?"

"Pretty good but I still have conditions to my 'gives'," said Teri.

"Easy. Flowed them right through," declared Sandra with confidence.

Turning his attention to Alice, Ling asked: "Alice? How are you doing?"

"Okay." She replied.

"Tough-one for you isn't it?"

"Yep."

"Want to talk it through?"

"Nope, same old crap." She replied and then continued. "I know that it's wrong but why can't my husband see all that I do for him? I just need him to meet me part way. I am changing everything for him and he just doesn't see it."

"Are you hearing your own words Alice?" Ling firmly asked.

"Yes. I am." she sighed sheepishly. "Not a lot of clean-giving. But he is so frustrating. I wish he could just understand me!"

"Keep trying to remove the expectation of him understanding you and just do the thing from love. Give unconditionally or tell him exactly what you need from him before you give. Keep working on it. It's not up to the other person to receive a gift with thanks - it's up to you to give it with 'thanks'."

Determined to bail Alice out, Peter decided it was his turn. He interrupted, "On the personal 'gives', I get it. Don't give something expecting something in return. But on a business front, that just isn't possible."

"Why's that Peter?" asked Ling sincerely.

"Because you need to have expectations. You need to have give-and-take. Otherwise the business will not thrive. How do you lead without expectations?" asked Peter.

"You are right Peter." Ling said.

"What do you mean? We can't both be right. I can't cleanly give without expectation and then have an expectation," Peter said becoming more frustrated.

"You are right again Peter," Ling said.

Holding his temper Peter thought: 'Argh, freaky old man. Do you know anything?' but instead said, "I'm sorry Ling, I'm confused."

"You are right that a business, and in fact, a marriage, a family, or a friendship, must all have expectations in order to 'thrive' as you say it. And you are right that you cannot 'clean-give', free of expectations and then place expectations on it." Ling calmly repeated Peter's words but then continued, "So you need to clearly articulate the expectation before the 'give'. Some things can be given without expectation, a candy, a hug, a present. And some cannot, such as an extension, a family holiday, a new house. Clean giving is about having everything "on-the-table" so the other party can cleanly receive."

Ling continued, "Giving cleanly is the cornerstone to living with integrity. Have you ever been given something, only later to find that there were hidden expectations and these expectations were actually valid but you just didn't know about them? That's what you are doing to others when you give something and expect them to react in a certain way. Giving cleanly is 'I can give you a two-day extension as it is important to the company that your report is thorough. Will two days ensure your report is stronger? Do you want to the two days knowing we expect a better report?' That is clean. Unclean is 'I know you have been working hard, take a couple extra days for the report.' Meanwhile you are fully expecting a stronger report. The first scenario allows that person to cleanly receive your gift or cleanly reject your gift. Make sense?"

"Yes, it does Ling," Peter replied. "Thanks."

Ling looked at everyone and said, "Okay, let's go back into meditation and receive cleanly. Close your eyes, center, ground, flow."

This got easier for Peter each time. The ball of light was back. He now understood the giving, and the receiving seems obvious.

"Receiving cleanly" Ling said, "is very simple. Receive a gift without strings. If you know or even sense there are strings attached, say 'no', get clarity, or sincerely thank them for the gift. Showing appreciation and gratitude for a gift is how abundance is created. For many people receiving a gift is not easy. We have been taught to either feel guilty for being given something or feel we must reciprocate the gift. Gratitude for a gift given empowers the universe to give more. A gift cleanly given to you is truly a gift, accept it and be gracious."

Ling paused for effect, then carried on, "Now think of the last gift you were given – whether it was that hug, a meal made by your spouse, or an extra effort from an employee. Did you receive it cleanly? Did you say 'What do they want?' or 'What do I need to do in return?' or did you sincerely say thank you, acknowledge the gift and show true appreciation?"

For Peter, a picture from years ago appeared. He was given a bonus in his younger years and he remembered how it made him feel. He remembered saying to himself: 'About time' and 'Is that all?' Now in meditation, he grasped that he hadn't receive that too cleanly. His throat and chest instantly tightened but he struggled to remember what those chakras meant. He guessed at communication and love/affinity and confirmed that this made sense. He knew he should have said something in that moment and that his reaction to that long-ago gift probably hurt the giver's feelings.

"Work through it" said Ling.

Peter pushed through the image, trying to increase his energy. Staying as grounded as possible, he focused on his throat and chest. The pain subsided as he imagined sincere regret and absolute gratitude.

"When you are ready, open your eyes and come out of meditation," said Ling.

Peter came out of meditation quite content, feeling as though a weight had been lifted - a weight he hadn't even known he was carrying. 'How many of these do I have attached to me?' he asked himself.

"How was that?" Ling asked the group.

"Good." Peter jumped in quickly. "I didn't realize how receiving a gift without gratitude even if it was sincerely given, can linger with you. I recalled a gift I was given 25 years ago. I've been holding that since then?"

"Yes, that's how it works Peter. And you probably give and receive with that cord still attached to you. Many cords are attached to us all. Lesson 26 takes care of these. For now, focus on the next gift you receive. Accept it cleanly, ask for clarity, or reject it graciously."

"Thanks, Ling" Peter replied.

"Anyone else want to share?" Ling asked.

Teri stepped up. "I still have a hard time saying no when I know it is not a clean gift."

"Yes, that is difficult. A wise woman once told me 'If it is not an absolute yes, then it has to be a no.' so be sure you can be grateful for the gift or it will weigh on you or knock you off your path."

"I'll keep trying," Teri replied.

The other two ladies shook their heads as Ling looked at them.

With that Ling said a few more words and wrapped up the session. Today had been very powerful for Peter. On Peter's drive back home his mind was calm and his thoughts were succinct: 'I am truly understanding that it is more than just clearing the mind of the clutter. I need to remember that everything is connected. Not sure I have felt this way before. I like it.'

Ling HO – MEDITATION

MASTER TEACHINGS

Lesson One

- See ball of light and move into center of heart.
- Connect cord from butt to earth.

Lesson Two

- Do lesson one over again.
- Focus on what is behind what you see.
- Block other things out and notice.
- Watch how people act and hear the words that come to mind.

- Be attuned to where on your body you feel something when the descriptors come up.
- Do <u>NOT</u> judge (very hard).
- Be aware that many things are happening at the same time as you are happening.

BE IN THE MOMENT

Lesson Three – CHAKRAS

Big lesson today! Gut feeling, headaches, control.

- Your personal space is the only circle of control.
- The personal space (aka aura) is an arms length around your body.
- Energy flows up from ground, down from universe.
- My personal energy flows around me and through my "CHAKRAS".
- 7 Chakras
    - 1st – privates - survival
    - 2nd – belly button - emotions & sensuality/sexuality
    - 3rd - solar plexus – gut feeling, purpose, control
    - 4th – heart – love others & self
    - 5th – throat – communication
    - 6th – forehead – clairvoyance
    - 7th – top of head – knowingness, enlightenment
- When I feel something like a lump in my throat I first acknowledge the feeling, try to understand it and then

move it through my body and down my grounding. *ASK Ling MORE*

- Thinking can lead to justifying. True answer is usually in first feeling.
- When I control my space and clear everything out I will then be able to find the answer.

Lesson Four

- Put thoughts in a container and destroy the container?
- Put dreams in a balloon and let them go?
- Realize you are crazy!

Lesson Five

- Take the time to look at the people you work with. Give them time to process their emotions.
- Understand their situation, see how that reflects in your own situation.
- LEAD through empowerment. Have them use their energy towards the goal.
- Create a vision of what you want and if it's in the "highest integrity" let it go.

Lesson Six

- Highest integrity of the universe is just that, acting in the highest personal integrity of everything around you.
- Acting as egoless as possible.
- Ego-based actions will give faster results, more "things" and quicker pleasures but it will also be short lived and the downside/fall is painful.
- Integrity-based actions will provide lasting results, more abundance and allow me to feel the ups and downs as part of a process to the journey.
- Mock-ups that are in line with integrity will have the aid of the universe (people, environmental, lack, etc.)
- Mock-ups that are ego-based will have the universe working against you or not at all.
- Try a mock-up with integrity while meditating.

Lesson Seven

- To have integrity one must give cleanly and receive cleanly. Having an unspoken expectation is a guaranteed way to be disappointed.
- Showing sincere gratitude for a gift given to you or giving a gift with sincere gratitude will attract peacefulness and even abundance.
- Say no unless you are sure it is a yes. But be gracious and clear.

- Do not give a gift with strings.
- Do not receive a gift with strings.
- Work through past mis-givings and mis-receivings while in meditation.
- Ask Ling if that's Karma.

Chapter Thirteen – Meeting in the Cafe

"I've decided I won't hand over the signing authority just yet Peter." Tim declared in a café full of people.

Peter sat without moving. His eyes looked around the room, but his body was in a frozen state. "Pardon?" He stared at his former employee. Tim had not been in the office for weeks and had continually delayed this meeting.

"I spoke with my people and we feel that until a few more conditions are met, I will remain in signing authority. It's no big deal, I will come in every once in a while and sign cheques and we can meet like this any time you want." Tim spoke as if this was a decision about paper clips.

Peter was now the witness to this event. He sensed that all time has stopped and he could see the entire room without moving. Tim's forced retirement appeared to fit him well. His white hair was wavy and long, and a white linen shirt and khaki pants rounded out the quintessential retirement look. The café was full, baristas were busy keeping up with the patrons. The four women at the table to his left were having a business meeting too and their papers were encroaching on Peter's seat. The guy to his right was reading the morning paper and drinking a very large latte. Peter saw two exits from the establishment, but wasn't sure yet why he'd noticed them.

"Large soy cappuccino for Peter" the barista's voice ripped into Peter's concentration.

Peter didn't move for what seemed like minutes, but was actually only a few seconds. He got up without saying a word and calmly retrieved his order. Methodically, he went to the prep station to add honey. He never added honey, but he took this moment to slow things down. To him, honey was slow. Stirring the morning nectar slowly but thoroughly, Peter finished and returned to the table.

"Are you ordering anything Tim?" Peter spoke without emotion.

"No I won't be here long." Tim replied.

With a huge breath in and a slow release, Peter began, "What you're suggesting is not what we agreed to Tim."

"Well we didn't actually agree." Tim replied. "I said there were a couple of things I wanted to talk to you about, but they weren't going to be a big deal."

"Actually we did agree and there are documents to support that." Peter said.

"I'm not going to be in the way of running the company," said Tim. "It's just easier for me to have that connection. You have to understand this is my retirement fund."

He slid a list of conditions across the table to Peter.

Peter didn't even acknowledge the piece of paper - he just looked Tim in the eyes in complete disbelief. His peripheral vision told him, however, that the list wasn't small. After a few seconds, Peter looked down, read each item and let out a disgusted laugh, "Tim, we've addressed most of these already and the new ones are irrelevant." The words hung in the air as Peter stood up, turned and walked out, leaving the piece of paper on the table.

Walking back to car, Peter was no longer capable of being in the moment. The last few months had all been for nothing. He had wasted his time and should have listened to Marie who told him Tim would never leave. Mindlessly Peter drove home, making turns but never actually being aware of them. His mind was pre-occupied with that internal conversation again, 'What have I done to deserve this? Tell me, what? How is this possible? I am left with no choice. I have to walk away. I have to let the company die and with it hundreds of thousands of dollars that won't be paid to vendors. Employees will be without jobs and the vision of the company I have for my family will be turned off. But business is business and folding the company is just a part of business. I tried, hell, I've tried too hard.' The proverbial last straw had landed on Peter's back. He picked up the phone and called his lawyer Henry who'd been in the loop on all the agreements. He left Henry a simple message: 'Hi Henry, it's Peter. Time to wrap this up. I'm moving on."

Chapter Fourteen – Karma in Action

Frustrated from the morning's events, Peter wanted to know what he'd done to deserve the difficulties he faced with Tim. He couldn't wait to ask Ling if this was Karma, so he went back to Google and typed in: *"What is Karma?"* He saw more than 64,500,000 results? Deja vu.

He read a couple of the top results.

'Karma is neither good nor bad, it just is. There is no good karma, nor is there bad karma, there just is karma.'

'Karma is the resulting existence of a past event. The cause and effect philosophy. Your existence today is the result of an action you took in the past, either in this lifetime or a past life.'

"Past life?" Peter said out loud. "Where am I going with this? Not sure I believe in past lives, so I'll stick to this life thank you, this one is tough enough!"

He read on;

'Each situation you face today is a karmic situation. Luck is non-existent. Good luck is the result of doing good-deeds. Bad luck is the result of doing bad-deeds. Continued misfortune is due to past lives of bad-deeds.'

"Yeesh," Peter said, "not sure I'm in agreement with this."

He decided to shut the computer down as the process clearly wasn't helping him. After fifteen minutes of thinking that he was result of his past life, he decided to call Ling.

"Hello, Ling?"

"Yes, Peter."

"How'd you know it was me? You always freak me out."

"Call-display, Peter."

Laughing, Peter replied, "Oh, yeah." Knowing not to say 'sorry', he continued. "I hope I didn't bother you but I have a question."

"No bother, Peter. What's your question?"

"After our last session about clean giving and receiving, I made a note to ask 'Is that Karma?'"

"Great question, Peter," Ling replied. "No, it is different from Karma. Clean giving and receiving is the logical cause and effect of a single action. Karma is a deeper, longer term cause and effect, even between lifetimes." Pausing to let that sink in, he then moved on, "That being said, Karma takes your actions as a framework for future situations. So not only will you benefit from, or pay for, your actions of today, these actions will also impact your future."

"Not sure I understand Ling," said Peter.

"Peter, we are in a cyclic existence until we break the pattern. We are all given opportunities each moment of each day. We choose whether we seize that opportunity or let it slip by."

The silence on the phone reiterated that Peter didn't understand.

Ling tried to dumb it down further, "Okay Peter, here's a scenario. See if you can comprehend the difference. Clean giving: You give everyone Friday off as they've worked hard. You tell them that you understand that no work will get done and you do not expect them to work eight hours more next week to make up for it, you truly feel they deserve a day off. By the end of the month they have exceeded goals for productivity as a result. Unclean giving: You give everyone Friday off, but give no clarification. Then, at month's end, when you miss productivity goals, you ream them out and say how disappointed you are. Is that part clear?" Ling asked.

"Yes, that I understand and I've actually experienced both those scenarios, so I get the concept," Peter replied with confidence.

"Okay, well Karma is when you are given this same scenario over and over again and you don't realize the difference before you react. You are experiencing Karma, Peter. You are not getting the message about how to give cleanly and act in the highest integrity of the universe. Karma is your cyclical existence and it is different by scenario or by person/spirit. We can dig deeper into this subject another time, but for today view it as this: sometimes you have a Karmic connection to a scenario or person and unless you change how you act, each time you interact with them, the scenario will be the same. Is there one person with whom you always act a certain way, even though you know it is not in the best interest of your 'mock-up'?"

"Ah? Yes, I guess I do." Peter sheepishly said, remembering all the past interactions with Tim.

"Well, until you break that pattern, you will live in that Karmic, cyclic existence. Karma is the result of actions you have taken in the past. It is not a direct cause and effect, but it is a cause and effect that transcends time. If it is the result of good actions, you will find the path easy and inspiring. If it was the result of bad actions, you will find challenges and detours along the way. You can't just ignore it or walk away. You must face the scenario and act. Simply meditate on it, clarify intentions, reset the desire to the highest integrity of the universe and envision the new result. Then, when presented with the scenario, take the highest integrity route no matter how painful. This route is not always rainbows and butterflies, and sometimes other people may feel you are not acting in integrity as they only have one vantage point. You know this scenario will repeat, and you must break it. You may be judged by many for acting as you are, but if you know it is in the highest integrity of the universe, their judgement has no weight. This route will help clear the past. Depending on the strength of the scenario, it may still repeat itself, so you must continue to take the "high road" again until that scenario stops presenting itself."

"I'm not sure I fully understand but it does resonate somewhat," Peter replied, feeling the deep pain of his current scenario.

"Just remember that if you want to have a different result from an experience that continues to present itself, take the road of integrity. Eventually the challenge will stop presenting itself, or at the very least you will understand it is not a challenge at all, merely part of the journey."

"Thanks Ling, I will try." Peter replied softly and sincerely.

"No problem Peter. That's part of fulfilling my Karmic contract with you!" said Ling.

And with that mysterious answer, they disconnected.

Ling HO – MEDITATION

MASTER TEACHINGS

Lesson One

- See ball of light and move into center of heart.

- Connect cord from butt to earth.

Lesson Two

- Do lesson one over again.
- Focus on what is behind what you see.
- Block other things out and notice.
- Watch how people act and hear the words that come to mind.
- Be attuned to where on your body you feel something when the descriptors come up.
- Do NOT judge (very hard).
- Be aware that many things are happening at the same time as you are happening.

BE IN THE MOMENT

Lesson Three – CHAKRAS

Big lesson today! Gut feeling, headaches, control.

- Your personal space is the only circle of control.
- The personal space (aka aura) surrounds body like an energy field approximately an arm's length around body.
- Energy flows up from ground, down from universe.
- My personal energy flows around me and through my "CHAKRAS".
- 7 Chakras
    - 1st – privates - survival

    - 2nd – belly button - emotions & sensuality/sexuality
    - 3rd - solar plexus – gut feeling, purpose, control
    - 4th – heart – love others & self
    - 5th – throat – communication
    - 6th – forehead – clairvoyance
    - 7th – top of head – knowingness, enlightenment

- When I feel something like a lump in my throat I first acknowledge the feeling, try to understand it and then move it through my body and down my grounding. *ASK Ling MORE*
- Thinking can lead to justifying. True answer is usually in first feeling.
- When I control my space and clear everything out I will then be able to find the answer.

Lesson Four

- Put thoughts in a container and destroy the container?
- Put dreams in a balloon and let them go?
- Realize you are crazy!

Lesson Five

- Take the time to look at the people you work with. Give them time to process their emotions.

- Understand their situation, see how that reflects in your own situation.
- LEAD through empowerment. Have them use their energy towards the goal.
- Create a vision of what you want and if it's in the "highest integrity" let it go.

Lesson Six

- Highest integrity of the universe is just that, acting in the highest personal integrity of everything around you.
- Acting as egoless as possible.
- Ego-based actions will give faster results, more "things" and quicker pleasures but it will also be short lived and the downside/fall is painful.
- Integrity-based actions will provide lasting results, more abundance and allow me to feel the ups and downs as part of a process to the journey.
- Mock-ups that are in line with integrity will have the aid of the universe (people, environmental, lack, etc.)
- Mock-ups that are ego-based will have the universe working against you or not at all.
- Try a mock-up with integrity while meditating.

Lesson Seven

- To have integrity one must give clearly and receive cleanly. Having an unspoken expectation is a for sure way to be disappointed.
- Showing sincere gratitude for a gift given to you or giving a gift with sincere gratitude will attract peacefulness and even abundance.
- Say no unless you are sure it is a yes. But be gracious and clear.
- Do not give a gift with strings.
- Do not receive a gift with strings.
- Work through past mis-givings and mis-receivings while in meditation.
- Ask Ling is that Karma?

Lesson Eight

- Karma is the result of actions in the past.
- Clean giving and receiving are in line with integrity.
- Cyclic existence is reliving the same situation over and over again.
- Every action we take today, shapes our path for the future.
- Acting with integrity will help stop the cycle of events.
- "Remember the deal that seemed to never end."

Chapter Fifteen– Being in the Moment

A couple of weeks had gone by since Ling and Peter had met. Being busy got the better of both men. Peter had been diligently trying to act with integrity but found it was sometimes difficult to determine. Wrapping up the company he knew was not in the highest integrity of the Universe, but staying in something without a plan for improvement was not in his or his family's best interests. Tim was in and out of the business and causing strain amongst the staff. Peter attempted to use Ling's teachings and at times it really worked. He was definitely noticing a difference in how people approached him. Some were more aggressive, trying to drive out the competitive killer in him and others were softer and much more agreeable. One thing for certain though, was that Ling's teachings kept him sane.

As Peter enters Ling's building, he noticed the stairwell once again. Same carpet, same missing gold thing, same extra step on the 3rd floor.

"Truly, what is up with that?" Peter asked out loud.

Peter opened the door and there was Ling, with a grin on his face.

"What's going on Ling?" Peter asked.

"I love Lesson Nine!" he replied.

"Okay?", Peter said, which really meant: 'You still are a bit freaky, old man.'

"Come, sit." Ling gestured with his hand to the same three chairs where they'd first met. The tea was poured in three cups, three cookies were on the plates. Ling locked the door and puts up the 'Be Back in One Hour' sign.

"Would you like some tea, Peter?" Ling asked.

"Absolutely," he replied, thinking that since it had been poured, he didn't see an option.

Ling's smile had not left his face. He was giddy - like a little kid on Christmas Eve.

"So why do you love Lesson Nine?" Peter asked, not really wanting to know the answer.

"Because it's the lesson before Ten and that's when I get paid, ha!" He broke out into a full belly laugh.

Peter was drawn in by his humor and couldn't help laughing himself.

"Just joking, Peter. I like Lesson Nine because today is the day you get a chance to 'Be' and I love to watch people BE."

"Sounds great, Ling, let's get to it then so I can give you more reasons to smile."

"You already have, Peter," he said. "Close your eyes."

Peter followed the commands now without hesitation. His new instincts told him to ground and center and go into meditation.

Ling didn't say his usual 'ball of light, center of heart, grounding cord, aura, etc'. He simply began, "List for me 15 things you saw in the room."

"Three tea cups 3/4 full of tea, three plates, three cookies, slightly overcooked," Peter said with a smile. "Dolphin print over your right shoulder, purple crystal on the shelf, a shelf," he continued, knowing that he should be 'looking' and not just trying to prove to Ling that he could list 15 things. "A shelf made of quarter-sawn mahogany, approximately three-feet long held up by two ornate grey shelf brackets, a loose thread on the empty chair, a smile on a friend's face seemingly caused by an expectation of lesson results," Peter threw that in for effect. "An old tea pot worn heavily on the handle with a chip on the base the size of a pea... I think that's 15." Peter proclaimed taking full advantage of the three cups, plates and cookies as nine.

"Very good, Peter. Open your eyes," Ling said.

"Thanks Ling, that was fun," Peter said. "I felt like a detective trying to explore the scene of a crime."

"That is today's lesson, Peter. 'Being.' Taking everything you have learned combined with your own personal power and then just 'being'. Today you will be the witness to everything that happens for the next 45 minutes."

"Cool!" Peter exclaimed, now excited about the lesson as well. "Let's start."

"Okay. Close your eyes, Imagine a ball of light Peter. It is a bright light. Imagine that ball of light out in front of you. Move it into the center of your heart. When you have that, imagine your grounding cord. A cord connected from the base of your spine to the center of the earth. Hook in the cable. Ground yourself. Make sure it is flowing. See the flow. Do not judge it, just make sure it is flowing down your grounding cord. Now clear your space." Ling uses his usual words this time, "You must completely clear your mind. Create the container, Peter. Put all your thoughts in it. All the experiences of last week, last two weeks, of our eleven weeks together. Put it in and destroy it. Keep creating and destroying them until you have no more thoughts."

Peter spent several minutes clearing his mind until he was sitting proud in his chair. Ling took that as the sign to begin, "Okay, one sense at a time. Be the witness in the moment. The moment is happening all around you,"

"Okay," he replied. "Which sense first?"

"That is your decision, Peter. You get to 'BE'," said Ling. "I'm leaving and going to my office to work. Here is a pad and pen if you feel you need to write down all that you sense."

Peter opened his eyes to see if Ling was joking but he was gone, walking down the hallway. Laughing to himself, Peter began with hearing. Closing his eyes again, he got centered and grounded and focused all his energy and attention on his ears. He heard the buzz of the air conditioner...the water fountain in the entrance...another buzz of an appliance...footsteps above...the creak of the walls...a fire truck, or was that a police car?...a horn honking...the laughter of passersby...a dog...a light bulb...a dripping faucet...Ling shuffling papers...keyboard strokes...a phone ringing.

Peter continued to build the list then switched to smell and a whole new world appeared. This place smelled great. The smells kept coming. As he labeled one, another appeared.

Taste was next. He took the time to 'taste' the cookie. Overcooked was wrong, it was delicious. The tea he took sip-by-sip, describing it in his mind. He would have liked to try some water on the cabinet, and that required him to move. He decided to leave the chair so he could actually sense the water. Next he tried a mint at reception. He found amusement and pride in actually experiencing a myriad of tastes in one room.

While up and walking around, he kicked into his sense of sight. At the same time he decided to map the room in preparation for the next sense - touch. Seeing much more detail than ever before, he took a good minute simply to look at a piece of furniture. He found the pictures of Ling and the powerful people on the wall again and looked deep into the images. He knew he could feel this way now. He got it. He pulled up a chair to the window and watched, actually witnessed, what was going on outside.

Feeling complete with sight, Peter shut his eyes and tried the sense of touch. Tactile surfaces were everywhere. He didn't even move for what seemed like 15 minutes, just touching things to understand each item without opening his eyes. He began to walk, trusting the map he created only a few minutes ago. There were a couple of stumbles, but he made it through, touching walls and doorknobs to get his bearings. He found himself at an open door and deduced that this was Ling's office. He opened his eyes to validate the map and there was Ling, smiling with great glee.

"Having fun, Peter?" Ling asked.

"Actually, yes I am," he replied. "Has it been 45 minutes?"

"Not quite," Ling answered, still smiling. "It's been 93 minutes."

"What!?" Peter exclaimed.

"Yep, you've 'been' for an hour and a half. How's the list coming along?" Ling asked.

"I felt I didn't need to write it down to 'be', because the moment I sensed that item, the moment passed. I experienced it and then moved on. I didn't care about the list. It wasn't a game just to get the most. It was... well, just being."

"Very good, Peter," Ling said with pride. "Very good."

"Thanks, Ling."

"My pleasure, Peter, because I had a chance to witness you being in the moment with an absolutely still mind."

"That was a great feeling."

"It is something you should do each day, even if it is for only two minutes. Just be. You now have access to the skills to shut out the chatter in your head. Use them."

"Thanks," Peter replied. "I will."

"See you next week! It's payday!" Ling said with a laugh.

"A well-deserved payday," Peter replied shaking his hand and bowing with respect.

That evening Peter pulled out his pad and reread everything he'd written to date and added today's lesson.

Ling HO – MEDITATION

MASTER TEACHINGS

Lesson One

- See ball of light and move into center of heart.
- Connect cord from butt to earth.

Lesson Two

- Do lesson one over again.
- Focus on what is behind what you see.
- Block other things out and notice.
- Watch how people act and hear the words that come to mind.
- Be attuned to where on your body you feel something when the descriptors come up.
- Do NOT judge (very hard).
- Be aware that many things are happening at the same time as you are happening.

BE IN THE MOMENT

Lesson Three – CHAKRAS

Big lesson today! Gut feeling, headaches, control.

- Your personal space is the only circle of control.
- The personal space (aka aura) is an arms length around your body
- Energy flows up from ground, down from universe.
- My personal energy flows around me and through my "CHAKRAS".
- 7 Chakras
    - 1st – privates - survival
    - 2nd – belly button - emotions & sensuality/sexuality
    - 3rd - solar plexus – gut feeling, purpose, control

  - 4th – heart – love others & self
  - 5th – throat – communication
  - 6th – forehead – clairvoyance
  - 7th – top of head – knowingness, enlightenment

- When I feel something like a lump in my throat I first acknowledge the feeling, try to understand it and then move it through my body and down my grounding. *ASK Ling MORE*
- Thinking can lead to justifying. True answer is usually in first feeling.
- When I control my space and clear everything out I will then be able to find the answer.

Lesson Four

- Put thoughts in a container and destroy the container?
- Put dreams in a balloon and let them go?
- Realize you are crazy!

Lesson Five

- Take the time to look at the people you work with. Give them time to process their emotions.
- Understand their situation, see how that reflects in your own situation.

- LEAD through empowerment. Have them use their energy towards the goal.
- Create a vision of what you want and if it's in the "highest integrity" let it go.

Lesson Six

- Highest integrity of the universe is just that, acting in the highest personal integrity of everything around you.
- Acting as egoless as possible.
- Ego-based actions will give faster results, more "things" and quicker pleasures but it will also be short lived and the downside/fall is painful.
- Integrity-based actions will provide lasting results, more abundance and allow me to feel the ups and downs as part of a process to the journey.
- Mock-ups that are in line with integrity will have the aid of the universe (people, environmental, lack, etc.)
- Mock-ups that are ego-based will have the universe working against you or not at all.
- Try a mock-up with integrity while meditating.

Lesson Seven

- To have integrity one must give cleanly and receive cleanly. Having an unspoken expectation is a for sure way to be disappointed.
- Showing sincere gratitude for a gift given to you or giving a gift with sincere gratitude will attract peacefulness and even abundance.
- Say no unless you are sure it is a yes. But be gracious and clear.
- Do not give a gift with strings.
- Do not receive a gift with strings.
- Work through past mis-givings and mis-receivings while in meditation.
- Ask Ling is that Karma?

Lesson Eight

- Karma is the result of actions in the past.
- Clean giving and receiving are in line with integrity.
- Cyclic existence is reliving the same situation over and over again.
- Every action we take today shapes our path for the future.
- Acting with integrity will help stop the cycle of events.
- “Remember the deal that seemed to never end.”

Lesson Nine

- Focus your attention on one sense at a time.
- Be a witness to what is happening around you.
- Notice so much more about the moment.
- "Be."

Chapter Sixteen– The Question

"What a great week!" Peter said aloud as he drove back to Ling's. He couldn't get over how easy the week had been. Even when the proverbial fires were ablaze, his calmness made the fire fade as fast as it started. The only sadness he felt was knowing how many people were going to be hurt when he closed the business - including Tim and Tim's wife. But he hadn't come up with any other solution, so he was at peace with what would happen. He got to Ling's office with ease, parking was a breeze and the community was alive with energy.

"Gonna miss this place," he said as he started to climb the stairs. This time, he decided to stop at the 3rd floor as he needed to know why there was an extra step. Opening the door, he saw the obvious answer. Ductwork and piping were staring him in the face as he looked at the ceiling. "Makes sense now," he said with a smile. A man walking the corridor looked at him but Peter just smiled and said, "Curiosity got the better of me." He returned to the stairwell, ascended the remaining flights and entered Ling's office. Ling was conveniently at the reception desk. "Making out my receipt are you, Ling?" Peter smirked.

"Actually, I am," Ling said with the same smirk. "Got my money?"

"Hey, hey, don't cheap out on my last lesson, Ling. We agreed to 10 steps," Peter replied still smiling.

"I will cleanly give you your training and cleanly receive your payment. This I can assure you." And with that, Ling gestured to Peter to go into the hallway. "Go to the small room, Peter, please. I will be with you shortly."

Peter entered the room and sat in one of the two chairs that were facing each other. 'What a journey,' Peter said to himself, 'Twelve weeks ago I couldn't even cross the threshold, now I am at peace in a 6'x10' box.' He prepared himself for meditation, not needing Ling's help. Center, ground, aura, energy flow. He created and destroyed the drive, the stairs, and even the 3rd floor mystery.

Ling came in and sat in the other chair not saying a word. He went into meditation himself. The master and student sat in silence for about five minutes and then Ling began, "Hello Peter. Good week?"

"Not to judge it, but yes," Peter replied confidently.

"Good to hear," said Ling, smiling a Ling-freakish smile. He continued, "Today is Lesson 10. Do you remember why you came to see me?"

"Yes. To learn to shut off the noise so I can see how to save this company and get my partner to understand." Peter replied.

"Okay. Today we deliver on that intention," Ling replied. "Ready?"

"Yes," Peter calmly replied, but he already knew the answer. The company couldn't be saved and Tim would never understand.

"Let's go back into meditation and clean up all the thoughts." Ling began his usual routine. "Clear your mind, Peter."

"Clearing." Peter instantly replied.

"Now, let's bring up each lesson and review it. Lesson One: Meditation basics," said Ling.

"Grounding, centering, ball of light," Peter replied.

"Excellent. Lesson Two: Reading energy."

"Noticing people and what comes up for me when I see them."

"Lesson Three: Chakras."

"Understanding a feeling in my body; working to get through the emotion, and feel the emotion."

"Good. Lesson Four: Mock-ups."

"Creating a picture of what I want in the future with the highest integrity of the universe in mind."

"Lesson Five: Empowerment of others."

"Assessing another spirit's situation and empowering them rather than trying to control them."

"Very good. Lesson Six: Integrity and intention."

"Realizing that acting with integrity is the cornerstone to receiving universal help."

"Good. Lesson Seven: Giving and receiving cleanly."

"Ensuring expectations are clearly articulated or accepting that a result may not occur as you expect and be okay with that. Receiving a gift only if it is clean and you understand and accept the expectation."

"Nicely said. Lesson Eight: Karma."

"Yeah, still a tough one for me, but essentially changing the response to cyclical actions through acting with integrity. Knowing actions today have an immediate effect and a long term effect."

"That works. Lesson Nine: Being."

Peter smiled. "Shutting down the mind and focusing on the moment with all of your senses."

"Most exceptional, Peter," Ling said. "Now, Lesson 10... answering your questions."

"Great."

"Shut everything down. Put the other nine lessons in a container and destroy it."

"Okay."

"Now," said Ling. "Ask the question."

"How do I shut off the noise so I can clearly focus on what needs to be done, so I can see the steps to saving the company and ensure my partner understands?"

The two men sat quietly with that question.

"Do you have your answer?" Ling asked.

Peter thought carefully and assessed exactly what he was doing in the moment. "Yes, Ling!" he said. "I can shut out the noise by simply accepting that the noise is there - by understanding that the noise is part of the answer. That I am actually living the answer. It is the journey I am on right now. Every step I have made, every mistake, every win, every unclean act and every clean act is the answer. The economy will be as it is and if I can just 'see' what is happening around me and not judge it, the challenges will be easier to overcome and a path will appear sooner. Tomorrow is yet to come and if I live with integrity, I will stay on my path and experience both ups and downs – knowing consciously that the up is there and the down is there. Both are a part of the path. Accepting that what people understand or don't understand is not my concern if I have articulated the reality. Doing the best I can with every situation that arises by facing it with integrity. If I do that I will not worry about what I did yesterday as I will know I acted with integrity. The noise around me will have no distracting quality as it will become a source of information from which I will make the next decision. All happens as it should and it is up to me to make a decision with the information I have been presented."

"Very good, Peter," said Ling, "Very good!"

Peter was fully inspired to wrap this up now. He brought his pad with him to have Ling review his notes, but instead took the time to write in the tenth lesson.

Ling HO – MEDITATION

MASTER TEACHINGS

Lesson One

- See ball of light and move into center of heart.
- Connect cord from butt to earth.

Lesson Two

- Do lesson one over again.
- Focus on what is behind what you see.
- Block other things out and notice.
- Watch how people act and hear the words that come to mind.
- Be attuned to where on your body you feel something when the descriptors come up.

- Do NOT judge (very hard).
- Be aware that many things are happening at the same time as you are happening.

BE IN THE MOMENT

Lesson Three – CHAKRAS

Big lesson today! Gut feeling, headaches, control.

- Your personal space is the only circle of control.
- The personal space (aka aura) surrounds body like an energy field approximately an arm's length around body.
- Energy flows up from ground, down from universe.
- My personal energy flows around me and through my "CHAKRAS".
- 7 Chakras
    - 1st – privates - survival
    - 2nd – belly button - emotions & sensuality/sexuality
    - 3rd - solar plexus – gut feeling, purpose, control
    - 4th – heart – love others & self
    - 5th – throat – communication
    - 6th – forehead – clairvoyance
    - 7th – top of head – knowingness, enlightenment
- When I feel something like a lump in my throat I first acknowledge the feeling, try to understand it and then move it through my body and down my grounding. *ASK Ling MORE*

- Thinking can lead to justifying. True answer is usually in first feeling.
- When I control my space and clear everything out I will then be able to find the answer.

Lesson Four

- Put thoughts in a container and destroy the container?
- Put dreams in a balloon and let them go?
- Realize you are crazy!

Lesson Five

- Take the time to look at the people you work with. Give them time to process their emotions.
- Understand their situation, see how that reflects in your own situation.
- LEAD through empowerment. Have them use their energy towards the goal.
- Create a vision of what you want and if it's in the "highest integrity" let it go.

Lesson Six

- Highest integrity of the universe is just that, acting in the highest personal integrity of everything around you.

- Acting as egoless as possible.
- Ego-based actions will give faster results, more "things" and quicker pleasures but it will also be short lived and the downside/fall is painful.
- Integrity-based actions will provide lasting results, more abundance and allow me to feel the ups and downs as part of a process to the journey.
- Mock-ups that are in line with integrity will have the aid of the universe (people, environmental, lack, etc.)
- Mock-ups that are ego-based will have the universe working against you or not at all.
- Try a mock-up with integrity while meditating.

Lesson Seven

- To have integrity one must give clearly and receive cleanly. Having an unspoken expectation is a sure way to be disappointed.
- Showing sincere gratitude for a gift given to you or giving a gift with sincere gratitude will attract peacefulness and even abundance.
- Say no unless you are sure it is a yes. But be gracious and clear.
- Do not give a gift with strings.
- Do not receive a gift with strings.

- Work through past mis-givings and mis-receivings while in meditation.
- Ask Ling is that Karma?

Lesson Eight

- Karma is the result of actions in the past.
- Clean giving and receiving are in the line with integrity.
- Cyclic existence is reliving the same situation over and over again.
- Every action we take today, shapes our path for the future.
- Acting with integrity will help stop the cycle of events.
- "Remember the deal that seemed to never end."

Lesson Nine

- Focus your attention on one sense at a time.
- Be a witness to what is happening around you.
- Notice so much more about the moment.
- Be.

Lesson Ten

- Every step we take is one that guides us along our journey.

- Step with integrity and the answers will come easily.
- We cannot control how others react, but we can control how we react to their actions.
- The answers always come with the question.
- A path will present itself if it was meant to be.

Chapter Seventeen – The Payment

Elated at the praise from Ling, Peter sat for a few moments soaking it all in. Ling gave him the peace and quiet and went into a meditation himself. The sounds appeared to have vanished. The scents had dissipated. The moment was Peter's.

Peter finally opened his eyes and came out of meditation. Ling felt or heard his movement and did the same.

They sat for a second just smiling and then Peter said, "So you wanna get paid, I bet?"

"That would be nice," Ling said.

They made their way back to the front reception. Everything seemed so calm and quiet. Peter felt light and at ease.

Ling handed him the invoice for the second payment as agreed and Peter wrote the check for $2,500. But then he wrote a second one for $5,000 - the amount they'd agreed Peter would pay when he felt he had benefited from the teachings. He handed Ling both checks.

"What's this?" Ling asked.

"I have already received the benefits, Ling. It's the agreed upon amount. The last instalment." he replied.

"Thank you Peter, but it is not necessary to be so soon," said Ling.

"I know, but I am cleanly giving as I know the benefits have far exceeded the $10,000." Peter persistently pushed the checks back into Ling's hands.

Ling said, "I cannot accept this Peter unless I fully understand how this benefitted you."

Peter took a deep breath, looked around the room, exhaled and began, "Ling, I came to you looking to learn the skills to still my mind. I needed to find a way to shut out the outside noise so I could find an answer to saving this company as well as a way to force my partner to understand. In twelve weeks, not only did you teach me the basics of meditation, but you taught me that those two questions were too elementary."

Peter continued, "The company is worth saving and I am emotionally attached to its success. For the first time in all the years I have owned various companies, I saw this one as the last. It was a way to bring stability and that was more important than the product. I also sought a way to force Tim to understand but I now see that Tim was merely scared. He was afraid of what will come when he lets go, putting the trust for his remaining years in my hands was something I think he wanted to do, but just couldn't.

"I now realize that I have acted with integrity for quite some time, keeping the company alive longer than anyone expected, but I could not continue. Several weeks ago, I set in motion the receivership of the company and with that, everyone will lose. I felt it was time for Karma to act on Tim and I couldn't help what might come. The employees will lose their jobs, the vendors will lose what they are owed, I will lose my investment and Tim will lose his retirement. It is a decision I made because I can't see any other path. Though that act may not be in the highest integrity, it is well within my rights. Moreover, I felt and still feel I have done everything in my power to save the failing organization, but it is time for me to move on to the next deal."

Taking in another deep breath before he continued, "Since that decision, you have taught me I have not exhausted all options.

Tomorrow I am making one last phone call. During my meditation last night, a name came to me that I have not thought of in a very long time. I am going to call someone with whom I have not spoken with in 17 years. I am not sure I can find her number, or if it is valid, or if she is even still in this industry. When I last did business with her, I had the utmost respect for what she had done and I believe she respected what I had done."

Looking directly at Ling, Peter ended his explanation, "If the universe wants this to happen, then the call will make its way through and a potential new option will appear. And if not, then the path is set and I will be okay with that. I have acted with my best ability in my highest integrity."

Ling took the checks, shook Peter's hand and simply said, "Okay."

Chapter Eighteen – The Contract

After reliving those past few months of his life, Peter came out of this deep meditation. Though he knew his journey had started long before and would continue long after, he cherished those 12 weeks with Ling as well as the following few weeks working out the details of his decision.

The receivership agreement sat on his desk. He knew it was the easiest option. His advisers told him the receivership was within his rights and it would be more final, allowing him to move on. He just wasn't feeling good about it. Though it was a simple way to end it, he knew it wasn't in his highest integrity.

But Peter had made that phone call a few weeks ago and to his surprise, it went through. A meeting later ensued that brought together two people who had not seen each other in nearly two decades. The needs of their two companies seemed to be aligned and the timing was perfect. As Peter thought about how perfect the fit was, he couldn't help but imagine the universe aligning for this new agreement to manifest.

He had been waiting all day for the new contract and the lawyers said it was coming but there had been no sign of it yet. Then a calm smile came to Peter's face as a messenger arrived at the front reception. Hearing the receptionist thank the courier, he got up from his desk and made his way to the front. The envelope had arrived.

He knew the contents of the envelope but was not sure whether or not he wanted to open it. The 9x12 kraft envelope had the weight of a big agreement, a sign of the heavy legal billings and numerous clauses he would need to live up to. But more importantly, the envelope held a new path for him - a path that allowed him not only to act in the highest integrity of the universe, but also to provide a safe landing for the employees and products and even save Tim's retirement fund. What should have taken months of due diligence had been completed in a few weeks. Trust seemed to be apparent on both sides of the table and the pursuit of a mutually beneficial agreement had helped pave the way to the very envelope that sat in front of him.

Peter had to decide between the two options - a decision he had to make alone. Option 1: Closing the company. Option 2: Trying again in a new partnership. Either option meant the same to Peter financially so he couldn't use that to make the choice. The first option of closing the company was final, a lot easier and required little effort from him, other than the stroke of a pen. It did, unfortunately mean the end for the employees, the products and the vendors. The second option, which was the new contract in the envelope, would be a more difficult road. It was a new partnership that saves the employees and the products. But it would require him to work harder and he would need the trust and support of many to see it through. He would be working longer hours and would need to prove himself again. The decision seemed unbalanced.

Further, if he chose the second option, the karma he hoped Tim would face would not manifest as Tim's retirement would be saved with this agreement. Peter thought about that and his smile disappeared. Tim had caused great pain and frustration and Peter's anger wanted there to be repercussions. He realized that Tim might never see any good in it and would probably never say thank you, but Peter heard Ling's teachings and acknowledged that karma was not his to serve and that option two must be in clean giving.

Peter's smile returned as that very thought tipped the scales. This new path, this new contract, this second option was the right decision to make. He opened the envelope and flipped to the last page. In putting his pen to paper, Peter signed, knowing that the road he was now on would not be easy, but it was in an act of the highest integrity possible. The mock-up he set free months ago had begun to materialize.

He was able to still his mind, accept the noise and see clearly what needed to be seen.

Peter's mind was completely CLEAR.